*The Sylvania Waters Diary*

Noeline's diary tells all:

- How the Donaher family was chosen for the documentary

- What really happened during the filming

- How the family feel about the notoriety the series has brought them

- How Sylvania Waters has changed their lives – are they still together, or has the series caused a family breakdown?

The Sylvania Waters Diary . . . a compelling read.

# *The Sylvania Waters Diary*

## Noeline Donaher

**ORION**

Dedicated to Mums around the world,
especially to my Mother who has been
a treasure all my life

An Orion paperback
First published in Great Britain in 1993 by Orion Books Ltd,
Orion House, 5 Upper St Martin's Lane, London WC2H 9EA

A CIP catalogue record for this book is available from
the British Library.

ISBN I 85797 219 8

Printed and bound in Great Britain by
The Guernsey Press Co. Ltd, Guernsey,
Channel Islands

# Foreword

TO all the critics who have mocked me and said: I bet the next thing she does is to write a book, well, you are correct and there are a few reasons for it. One is to square off with my family, and another is to thank the hundreds of people who have written to me.

To these people — I thank you for your lovely letters, cards and flowers, which have meant so very much to me. My house has been full of flowers for weeks and the postman must wonder what has happened. This mail has come from all over Australia. One young person sent me a Bible, although I already have one. Even if it takes me forever, I will personally reply to everyone. To you all, I thank you for your support.

Oh, yes. There have been roughly seven dreadful 'letters' — so dreadful that I will reveal some of them throughout this book. It is easy for Laurie and Michael to say: 'Just burn them', but I have upset these people and please believe me, it was never meant to be this way.

Another very important reason for writing the book is to set the record straight on what *really* happened during the course of the filming and screening of *Sylvania Waters*.

In the three weeks prior to the series being aired we were criticised, humiliated and cursed by leading media people, but everyone has missed some very important points.

• We were told that this documentary series would not really be of great interest in Australia. Did you know that the name of the series was always going to be *The Family*? I also ask who supplied all this damaging information to the media? It was fed out by the ABC's Publicity Department, as at that stage I had given only one interview, and that was to Phil McLean of the *Sunday Telegraph*.

• Our surnames were not to be divulged at any stage and our addresses, as far as possible, were to be withheld. So what happened to this verbal contract we had with the ABC and BBC? It was Quentin Dempster, on the ABC's *7.30 Report* back in July, who first revealed both our surname and name of our street, and this has made us virtual prisoners within our home.

• In my opinion we were fed a pack of lies. The show was to promote Australia, not defame it. All I can say is that the taxpayers have paid dearly for this so-called documentary.

• If I were ever to come across our beloved BBC directors and producer I would most certainly retaliate. I'll be damned if I will allow them to be the reason why my family has been separated.

• When I place any form of advertisement in any paper I have to pay for it, and it is very expensive. I would like to ask who paid for the one and two page spreads that were run on our family? No-one had tapes of the show at that stage. I have since found out that all of this information came from the ABC Publicity Department and can only assume that a member of that department would watch the tape for the following week, then release the information to the papers. So, when you were all reading about how Noeline and Laurie were fighting over Michael's birthday, and that Noeline is a heavy drinker, all of this information was being given out by the ABC.

What a hell of a trick to play on anyone! I will never understand how these people smiled at our faces, but behind our backs they must have laughed all the way home.

It was a horrible thing to do, but the idea is plain to me now. Here was their golden opportunity to blatantly make an absolute monkey out of me — which is how a huge number of people saw the whole fiasco. We were so blind. Chris Pip, who originally made contact with us for the ABC, was either blind like us, or full of gall if she had any idea of what we were to encounter. I do not think for one moment that Chris was in on the deal, but her husband, Harry Bardwell from the ABC, told us that he had given information to the newspapers — meaning no harm, of course!

\* \* \*

Throughout my life I have tried to do my best for my family and friends. I have tried to be a good person, a good wife and a good mother and no-one has fully realised how I have felt over these past few months. No, I am not asking for any medals or for sympathy, for what is done can never be retrieved.

I have, through accepting the ABC's and BBC's contract, caused a rift that will be difficult to repair between my husband, Laurie, and my son, Paul. Perhaps, through this book, they will realise how very bad I feel about the whole ordeal. I ask them to understand that if I could have looked into a crystal ball I would never have considered doing what I did.

To my family — Laurie my husband; my children Paul, Joanne and Michael; my stepson Mick; to Dione and Kane, Yvette, Kristy and Lisa — this is from the bottom of my heart. I am just so sorry for everything and I can only hope that in time all the pain I solely have caused you will disappear. I wish that we could go on with life as it was before this incredible show *Sylvania Waters*, but I guess it has changed our lives forever.

# *My Story*

*I am about to tell you how* Sylvania
Waters *came about, but I feel that to
get started you should know who I
am and where I came from.*

I was born in New Zealand, in a little town called Inglewood, 15 miles from New Plymouth. I was the sixth of a family of nine children. My mother was amazing — she washed for us all by hand with a copper. No washing machine and no electric stove, but there was plenty of love for us kids. Dad drove a truck in those days and he used to have a drink in the pub every afternoon. He left it to my mother to train and educate us, be a fine doctor and nurse, and teach us about God. There were many times when her prayers could not have been heard — such as when Dad had planted the cabbages on a Sunday, and we played in the cabbage patch after school on Monday! My mother was a saint — bear in mind that if one kid got the measles or mumps, so did the others.

I went to school in Inglewood, in the days of school milk. I used to hate the half-pint of milk we'd all get: it was usually curdled or very sour. In those days my parents couldn't afford to buy us shoes, and I never got a new singlet. I got all the hand-me-downs. There were so many in our family that we practically made up the numbers for the entire school.

I loved my parents though, with the natural love that most normal kids have. I played with my brothers and became quite a tomboy, but could still be a little girl as well. One Christmas my Dad, bless his soul, made me a doll's pram which I thought was beautiful, but my brothers decided to use it as a billy cart. My pram, my pride and joy, became a wreck and being sixth in line I never got the doll to go with it. My kitten was a good substitute though.

And then there was Bunty. We all had a pet lamb from time to time and mine was Bunty — a very intelligent little creature. Just before Christmas one year Bunty disappeared and my life was shattered. Dad said he must have wandered off, but I knew he wouldn't have left me. On Christmas Day, there was Bunty on the table — my pet was our meal. I went to my room in tears.

I forgot to tell you that I was christened with two unforgettable names: Noeline Vera. How could any mother and father do this to a child? I was born with big feet and became so tall that you could find me in any crowd. So we have Noeline Vera with big feet and no shoes, a tomboy and growing fast to become 5 feet 10 inches tall.

My parents worked damned hard for us, probably too hard, and they had disputes just as you or I do. There was never enough money of course. Just paying the food bill for nine kids was no easy feat, but they managed by cutting corners on everything. When it was bathtime (and we bathed every day) the girls would top and tail, and the boys the same, to conserve water and electricity. My Dad even made the toothbrush rack with names that read Ian, Mervyn, Murray, Brian, Allan, Dad, Mum, Doreen, Annette, Margaret, Noeline. There's that awful name again.

I had a favourite sister, who would let me sleep in her bed when I was little if I was frightened of the dark. She'd go with me and hold my hand if I wanted to go to the toilet during the night. That wonderful older sister even taught me the facts of life, when I think about it. She would let me ride her bike to school, on the condition that I cleaned it and put it back in its place.

I was a normal young kid, with a normal capacity for natural love for her large family, and proud to be a part of it. I had a beaut life, but perhaps I grew up thinking that I knew better than anyone else.

Our upbringing was no different from anyone else's and we had our ups and downs. We never won prizes (I still cannot win Lotto), we went to church every Sunday (we'd put in sixpence and take out two shillings), and were just normal kids on the street. My mother used to have two favourite sayings: 'No wonder I drink', and 'One of these days I will pack my bags and walk out', and I've had these with me all my life. You could count my mother's drinks on one hand, and leave home she never did. They were just pet sayings of hers.

We later moved to New Plymouth and I was an average lanky kid who was full of life, playing silly games and pranks with my brothers and getting a belt on the backside when I misbehaved. By now I was at intermediate school and developing into a teenager. My worst memory of this time is of my girlfriend, Margaret Keightley, being taken by a shark at Oakura Beach. She was a very good friend: we sat together and had lunch together and so I knew very early on what it was like to lose someone close. A shark attack and my best friend dead: I was 12 years old and I was devastated. I had to bear the funeral and I remember asking God that night: 'Why? Why Margaret?' No answers of course. My Mum and Dad had some answers, but to a very sad and impressionable young girl they were hard to swallow.

Ashamed as I am of this at my stage of life, I learnt to smoke in those days. Yes, Mr Howe, smoke! We'd sit in a tree-house and roll up newspaper and light it. They certainly weren't proper cigarettes, but they had the same effect. They would burn down to your lips and then you'd cough and splutter and nearly choke yourself to death.

My father had worked so hard by this time that he had progressed from being a truck driver to a linotypist for the *Taranaki Daily News*. My parents had a mortgage with the AMP Society and for 27 years of their lives they paid the interest, and in the last nine years they paid off the house.

My first job (Dad commanded: 'You find a job before you leave school'.) was with a firm of accountants. I'd bring my pay packet home and Dad took half, and we were taught to save from the word go and not to have accounts. Dad would say that if you earn five pounds, you must save half for the future, but I'd spend my pay like water.

I did get myself into trouble with this. Mum was on good terms with the owners of a shop called Lucas's in the main street of New Plymouth. I used to go through nylon stockings like you wouldn't believe, so I went in and set up an account with them, assuring the people in the shop that my Mum and Dad knew about the arrangement. My charge account was going along fine until a bill was put in our letterbox. Was I in hot water! I paid the account hastily and promised never to do such a thing again, and I didn't.

For six months the senior lady, Shirley, taught me how to stamp the mail, walk to the Post Office, put the mail in the slot and then walk back and resume my duties as an office clerk. I hated walking to the Post Office, but I would take the opportunity of looking out of the side of my eye to see what talent was around — I was 15 by now. I also cleaned the toilets at work every Friday afternoon and after six months I had perfected all my duties.

And then I fell in love — I thought I was really grown up. I was in love with my first boyfriend and life was complete. The aim was to meet a guy, fall in love and buy a section (a block of land). Both sets of parents would get along well, then after a couple of years you would get engaged, and then married. His name was Bryan and in my mind he was perfect. Although I was very lanky, with those big feet, I was in love. He was mine and I was his and our life was going to be utter heaven. But that is not what his parents had in mind. They liked me a lot and allowed us to become involved, but the whole romance became too serious so they sent him off to Australia.

My life was over. I cried and cried and just couldn't get myself together, so what did I do? I took an overdose of Mum's sleeping tablets and went to bed, but they found me and called the family doctor who pumped my stomach out at the hospital. Shame, shame, shame. I was an insecure young adult at this stage, but my life was shattered. And I couldn't even commit suicide properly.

My everlasting love had gone to Australia, which to me in those days was on the other side of the world. There I was, still in New Zealand full of gloom and heartbreak, so my girl friends decided to take me away for a holiday to cheer me up. By now, nearly all of the girls were engaged or married and I was the ugly duckling with a broken heart and no place to go. But off to Nelson we all went for a holiday.

It was there that I met a young man from Australia (how ironic), who seemed to like me. A new romance started and some months later I was to marry my second love. I was in love again, and for me this was marriage for life.

We lived in Wellington for some time, and this is where my son Paul Anthony Eric Baker was born — a big, bouncing boy of 9 pounds 3 ounces. I was proud and elated, but childbirth was hell. Now there were three of us: quite a little family. My marriage, however, was very shaky from day one. We both worked very hard but were loving parents to our adorable son. I did dressmaking during the day and worked three nights a week as an usherette at a picture theatre. My husband worked all day as a labourer and went on to a cleaning job in the evenings. We also had a young lady who boarded with us, and this helped financially.

My husband later joined the New Zealand Police Force and we were sent to Rotorua, where he took up his first post. This is where my daughter, Joanne Marie Baker, was born. She was the dearest little baby who slept all day, no trouble at all.

We then moved to Australia and I was homesick for 18 months. I did have a new family though, and they were fabulous — my first father-in-law became my best and truest friend. I had another son after we moved to Australia: Michael Kevin Baker. He was an asthmatic and very sick for a long time, but I was so lucky to have the most wonderful three kids in the world.

A lot happened over these years, but with respect for my previous family I will finish there.

The shaky marriage that I have already spoken of was about to end. It was time for me to move on to the next stage of my life with my three children. I left the family home with just a small car, pillows and blankets and, with tremendous hesitation, moved into a half-house at Blakehurst in southern Sydney. I had nothing but a good job and three small children to feed, educate and keep together. It was so hard being a sole parent, but we made it. Every Thursday night after I got paid we would go to Hurstville and I'd buy one towel, or one sheet, out of my small budget. We had enough food, and we had one another.

I want you to understand that I was never a bludger. You have to be so very strong in such a situation and you learn very quickly to fight for everything you feel is right. A survivor is how I would describe myself.

I would put Michael into kindergarten, drive Paul and Joanne to school, then go to work. I'd ring in the afternoon to make sure Paul and Joanne had got home okay and give them chores to do. By the time I got home from work with Michael it was almost bedtime. Those were long days when I think about it now. The only thing in my favour was that I had a good job.

It was hard fighting for three children who needed love and a lot of attention. I have so much respect for any mother out there who is trying to survive and make ends meet as a sole parent. It is not easy. The children's wants and needs are so very important and the love that should come from two parents has to be provided by one. It is confusing to small children, but I did my best and they seemed quite well adjusted. Although I had to give more attention to Paul than Joanne and Michael, he seemed quite normal to me.

I would go out on some Friday nights (I have to be so careful here, or I will get into more trouble), and this is how I met Laurie, which I am sure you all want to hear about.

The night I saw Laurie, it was love at first sight. I had gone to a Rugby Union club at Hurstville, because I was bored with the same old people at the RSL club I had been going to for 12 months. Our eyes met the moment he walked through the door. He was so inebriated (I guess anything can look beautiful when you are inebriated!). He introduced himself to me and I was a little dubious, as he told me that he was divorced although he had two young boys. But I had to ask myself if someone with a face like Laurie's could tell a mistruth?

We danced and had a drink, then danced some more and he told me that I had big hands. He didn't dance real well, in fact he nearly broke all of my toes! He also said that I had lovely blue eyes and could he see me again sometime when he wasn't so drunk? He walked me to my car that first evening and we kissed in the doorway of Buttercup Bakeries. He made arrangements to pick me up the next evening for dinner. As we drove away in our different directions, I realised that he didn't have my address and that it would be impossible for him to find me. I wasn't even in the telephone directory.

He turned up at my door the next evening, much to my amazement. We had our first real night out and have been together since that time. That was 13 years ago and I still don't know how he found out where I lived.

Our best friend and office manager, Ron, tells a story about the night that Laurie met me. Laurie worked for Ron in his butcher's shop at Earlwood then and Ron arrived in the shop at 5.30 am on the Saturday morning to find his number-one offsider sleeping on the counter. On waking Laurie, Ron discovered that he was over the moon about having met this big blonde. Ron was a bit sceptical as Laurie thought any woman was beautiful when he was drunk, so he reserved his judgment until later.

Laurie never told me much about himself during those first few months, but as time went by I realised he had obviously been around. There weren't many places he hadn't been to in his 35 or so years and he certainly brought some excitement into my life. We went to places and did things that I had only read about: two-up schools, gambling clubs, trotting meetings, greyhound races, water-skiing, car racing. At all of these venues he would always know someone or other, and I would think: 'What have I got myself into here; this bloke is a bad man'. Not so. It appears that during Laurie's 20 years as a butcher in many parts of Sydney, he had discovered and gone to these places that he was now taking me to.

We never had any problems at these so-called 'houses of ill repute', and Laurie was always a gentleman. The closest we ever came to any trouble was at Thomo's two-up school in Oxford Street in the city. We arrived ten minutes after there had been an armed hold-up of the players by hoods with machine-guns.

From the events he has told me about, Laurie certainly hasn't been a saint all his life. I don't know how his first wife stayed with him for so long. Every now and then something from his past bobs up and he tells me the story. Just when I think I know all about him, there's more. I cannot understand some of the things that he did when he was younger. He was an only child, and

I am sure he was given everything by his parents, but that did not stop him from going out and taking from others. His biggest problem seemed to be cars (and still is). If he couldn't afford one himself, he would go out and take someone else's. One night his battery failed while he was out with a lady, so he just went around the corner and took a replacement from someone's car. Oh, he had so many tricks!

I know he spent a short period in jail; Long Bay, I think. This was to do with cars as well. He did have a fairly long record before I met him, but I can hopefully say that since we have been together he has never been in trouble with the police for anything other than a traffic offence. He also had a bit of a reputation with the ladies before we met, but hopefully I have managed to snap him out of that too.

My world was soon in turmoil again. I believed that Laurie was divorced, but after some time I discovered that he was married, and very much so: but I was in love for the third time in my life. We had no intention of meeting and getting together that night at the Rugby Union club, nor did we have any intention of hurting anyone. The hurt we delivered to others, though, was tragic and the anguish over the next few months was extreme. We had sent his household into chaos, his wife into a state of collapse and his children were so fearful of being hurt.

But we continued and moved in together — Laurie, myself and my three children. We were in love and happy and started a new life. Laurie was still a butcher and I worked for a company as a wage clerk, but over our romantic candlelit dinners we discussed how we could spend every moment together. This is how we started a business in the small suburb of Peakhurst — supplying contract labour hire to the metal trades industry.

By this time I had met Laurie's two boys, Mick and Stephen. Mick and I got along fine. Although I knew he was hurt, he accepted the situation for what it was. As for Stephen, we don't see much of him and with the greatest of respect for him I will leave it at that.

My son Paul did not really accept Laurie as being the head of our modest family. He didn't feel that anything Laurie and I did was of any benefit to him and he gave us some awful problems back then. It probably wasn't his fault. Although he was in agreement about the end of my marriage to his father, I am sure he was full of torment. This became very apparent over the next few years.

\* \* \*

There is something that I would like to say here — to Paul, in particular.

*To me, the price of divorce is devastating to the ones that are not involved, and these are the children. You get married, you think it is love, you build a family, you work and strive for happiness. But you and your partner become unhappy and you destroy each other's self-esteem. Before you know it, you have also destroyed the most important part of your life — your children.*

*I have committed this crime. I fell in love and had three children, but fell out of love when the chips were down and failed miserably. To the children it's a matter of Mum separating from Dad, starting a new life, then meeting Joe Blow — her second chance for happiness. But what about the kids; what do they really think of it all? They love both Mum and Dad, and they are forced to choose. They want Mum to be happy, but what about them? Always remember the children and how they feel. I have, I guess, destroyed the feelings in five children.*

*       *       *

Paul left us when we lived at Peakhurst. He didn't feel that he could comply with our 'rules' and went to live with a friend and his family down the road. This was to be his residence for some time. It was all very unfortunate, but he rebelled against any of our demands, if you can call them that, and he was very hard to live with. We just couldn't understand his attitude, and he couldn't comprehend ours. Anyway, Paul went on his merry way, so I sadly said farewell. We were left with Joanne and Michael, and Mick visited us often.

Laurie and I bought a second-hand car for Mick for his sixteenth birthday. It was a Valiant and we thought it was great, but Mick was not amused. He was way past the Valiant stage, for some reason or another. We also bought a station wagon for Paul, the best we could afford. It was a lovely one-owner car and we thought it would be perfect for him to go the surf, where he spent virtually every waking hour. Again, we chose incorrectly. He didn't want this car and eventually it was sold for scrap and the plates handed in for cash. We held a post-mortem and decided that though we had meant well, we just couldn't get it right with the kids.

At this stage my children had very little contact with their dad, who, by the way, never sent a birthday card, or any presents for birthdays or Christmas.

Laurie and I had Joanne and Michael and our business, which was running along very well — even if we worked hard for few rewards. Joanne felt, after Paul left, that our rules were more than she too could bear, so for a while she went to live with her father. He never spent a penny on any of them, but he couldn't stand Laurie and I making decisions about the children. This was a sort of punishment for both of us, as I believe Laurie cared very deeply for my three kids.

We struggled along with our contract labour business, saving every cent, but in 1982/3 the bottom was falling out of Australia and we decided to buy a run-down supermarket at St Peters. There were only a handful of men in our contract labour side of things, so we did both jobs. We would work all day at the supermarket until we were nearly dropping, then go home to do the office work and try to be good parents too.

It was so hard. My three kids were driving me mad. Joanne and Michael were at school and Paul, at this time, was unemployed and living with us again. He was so strict with the other two and there were constant phone calls to the supermarket saying: 'Paul is hitting me,' or 'Joanne won't do her homework'. It nearly sent Laurie and I berserk, but it wasn't the kids' fault that they were unsupervised early in the morning and late in the afternoon. The supermarket kept Laurie and I so busy, with the help of our part-timer, Laurie's dad Allan. We struggled and struggled to keep it all together, but something had to give. Although we instilled in the kids that this work we were commited to was for their future, it was hard for them to comprehend. Michael was only five years old.

We made the decision to put the supermarket up for sale, cut our losses, get out and come back home to try to repair the children's lives. You'd have to give Laurie 100 out of 100 for his part in this: he was just so good to my three kids. Once again, I will take the blame here. Perhaps I was too busy trying to succeed and not giving the children enough attention. Rather than have arguments I often gave in and spoilt them. Paul was out of control and left us once again to live away — to be honest, this cushioned Joanne and Michael somewhat.

My lovely Joanne was roughly 14 years old at this time and a very bright, positive and stubborn girl. She came home from school one day and explained to Laurie and I that a teacher had advised her she would be better off leaving school next year, and going out into the workforce. This caused a riot in our house. There was no workforce, the country was on its knees, and here was this teacher advising our Joanne to leave school. I rang the teacher to ask her to explain the reasons for this advice. She felt that Joanne would not learn anything more by staying at school. Joanne went back the following year, though, and got a mark of 246 in the HSC, which certainly proved a point to the teacher.

I am sure that in those days both Joanne and Paul would really have liked my relationship with Laurie to end. I often wonder how we survived the pressure, as they gave Laurie a very difficult time.

And then there was Michael, who adapted to Laurie like a fish to water. They were very close. I guess Michael has only ever known Laurie as a father figure, although he and Joanne do visit their natural father on rare occasions. Contrary to what was mentioned in *Sylvania Waters* by Paul, I have never known Laurie to raise a hand to my children. The most Paul ever received from Laurie was a push out the door when he was going to knock my block off over some argument we were having. I will not sit back and have Laurie accused or ridiculed, for he was and is a good, honest and very fair de facto stepfather. In my heart I knew that our love for each other was true, because any other man would have said goodbye long before then.

Laurie and I do have domestics. That is an understatement — we have some of the most horrific arguments, but you see we work together, live together and sleep together and we are both very strong-willed people who have different ideas. For instance, I am a Labor person: Laurie is not. I believe that Labor is the only way to go, although you will see later that I have recently re-thought this. However, we get along famously for, say, 16 hours of the day and do like the same things. If I can boast, I'd say we make a very good working team.

The first house we bought was in Sylvania, southern Sydney — this was our first big commitment to each other. We traded in a block of land and my car and scraped the rest of the money together to buy the house. We had to meet the owner on a Friday night to consolidate the deal, but were roughly $2000 short of the total figure. Being gamblers at heart, Laurie and the owner tossed for the $2000 and we won. Off we were, into our first proper home!

It was a lot of fun. Our wages went on paint and nails and such things every week — in fact, we would have been better off taking our wages straight down to BBC Hardware! We painted this and that, bought a second-hand stove and carpet from an ad in the paper, and within a short time the house was ready to move into. It was our pride and joy and we made a decision to put the racing car (racing was by now very much a part of our lives) away for 18 months, or until we had completed all the things we planned for our home.

We paved the large driveway — it was a mammoth task, but even the kids helped out. With positive thinking, and Laurie at the helm, we turned that little house into a beautiful home. Hard work keeps you going, don't you agree? It took us two years to create what we wanted and we loved the house. Laurie is very house-proud, clean and tidy and nothing annoyed him more than the children's untidy bedrooms. Paul would have to get full marks here though: he has always been neat and clean.

Although Laurie was a de facto father, no-one can say he was mean and horrible. He would always listen to my children's wants. When Joanne wanted her first car he told her we would put up half if she could save the rest. She did just that and Laurie found her a red Laser. Laurie did countless things for my children, but even at this point the most they showed him was hostility.

By now we had bought a boat and having it moored was somewhat of a pain, so in 1988 we decided to sell the house and move on to, yes you've guessed it — MacIntyre Crescent, Sylvania Waters. As you have seen, we could keep the boat right outside the house. The house was very liveable when we bought it, but we entertain a lot and have our families to cater for, so we worked hard, extending and renovating. Not everyone likes what we did, but we are very happy with the results.

This home is for everyone to enjoy, if they can behave themselves when they come here. We have a lot of fun at weekends, out at the pool area, or on the boat. And, contrary to all newspaper reports, our home is *not* up for sale.

We have had a few unexpected hurdles to overcome. Business is down compared with this time two years ago, and although we go to the office every day and work hard it is still difficult to make ends meet. Small businesses like ours are having a hard time in this recession and seem to be doomed, and without our business we stand to lose everything. We certainly could not afford to live here. Our critics will be gnashing their teeth by now, but although what we have may look very grand, it is not that easy. Building something up is relatively simple compared with maintaining it. All those hours we have toiled throughout our lives could still prove to have been in vain.

# Sylvania Waters

*Of course, what everyone wants to know is how did* Sylvania Waters *come about? Well, it all started at the end of October 1991.*

# The beginning

## October, 1991

ONE morning in late October, when I was sitting in the kitchen having a cup of tea, my attention was captivated by a conversation on 2KY radio station. It was Peter Peters talking to a lady called Chris Pip from the ABC, who was describing a documentary. She was looking for an interesting Australian family, who would allow a film crew to come into their home and film for five to six months, or whatever time would be needed to put a series together. Requirements: they had to be interesting, active and outgoing, and I was nearly positive I heard the amount of a quarter of a million dollars mentioned.

That sort of money would take care of a number of our financial problems and, oh yes, we were all of those things — interesting, active and outgoing. Joanne had gone to work and Michael to school and Laurie was sick in bed, so I wrote down the number on a piece of paper, put it in my handbag and went upstairs to hastily get ready for the office.

When I got to work we were busy: with Laurie out of action Ron, our office manager, and I had our hands full. But when things had returned to normal and Ron had gone on his way, out came the piece of paper, and yes, I dialled the number. Chris Pip answered the phone and before too long I had told her all about us and suggested that we should be the family to show the British how lucky we were to live in Australia. Why not my little clan? Chris made a time for us to meet on the following Tuesday and the next thing for me to do was to alert my extended family.

I started by ringing Joanne. We laughed about it, but Joanne kept saying: 'Mum, what have you done?' I comforted her by saying that we would probably never hear back from this lady. I rang the other girls. Yvette and Dione were not as alarmed as Joanne — in fact they just giggled. None of us thought it would come about, and hell, I still had Laurie to tell. What was I going to say to him? I arrived home and went upstairs to find Laurie sound asleep, so I opened and shut a few drawers and finally he woke up. I sat on the bed and told him. You must remember that I was thinking of a $250,000 fee, so his response was very good and that was where it ended until the following Tuesday.

# November, 1991

Tuesday evening arrived and the entire family had descended on our home. For the next few hours we talked to Chris who, by the way, is a super lady. She took still photos of us and did a little videoing and at this stage no-one asked about money. But she was full of ideas and asked a lot of questions like: 'Do you go out in your boat much?', 'Oh, you go car racing? How interesting.' She asked how old we were, did we snore, did we have bad habits and we got through this first interview. Chris also went next door, as we are very good friends with our neighbours, the Wicks. She chatted to them, explaining generally what she was after and what would be required.

Chris called me again at work on the Thursday morning to say that the ABC director was besotted with our family. We had all come up well in the video and we could expect to hear from her in a few days. The director rang the same day and I felt that she too had made the decision that it was going to be our family. Before the big chief from the BBC came over from London she wanted to film a bit more footage.

So Chris had lunch with Joanne and went to school with Michael, although she was only permitted to go to the gates. Because all this was being done we felt sure we had been chosen as the family who would represent Australia, and that the documentary series was about to commence. Everyone in the family was very intrigued, and yes, a sense of stardom had hit most of us. We were going to be on television! Bear in mind that we thought we would be getting this huge amount of money and become instant movie stars. Oh dear, how stupid and naive it was when I look back on it now.

# December, 1991

Mr Paul Watson, the BBC producer, arrived in Sydney and he came out to the house and talked to Laurie and myself without the kids around. He outlined what he was looking for and said that it was a documentary series and he could see it being highly successful. (Ho, ho, ho! ) After a series of phone calls it was arranged that we would meet the rest of the crew for dinner — the two BBC directors, Kate Woods and Brian Hill, and a whole lot of other people from both the ABC and BBC.

# 5 December, 1991

Dinner was very successful and they spent the night moving around the table talking to each of us. Then the bomb dropped. Laurie asked the burning question of: How much do we get? All hell broke out. Laurie nearly swallowed his glass; Joanne went white with rage and got up and whispered in my ear: Count me out for that sort of money. Just count me out. The people in the restaurant must have wondered what had gone wrong. Here was this enormous crowd having a lovely time, then the next few hours turned into complete chaos.

By now, Laurie was at another table with Mr Watson and a director from the ABC. Mick was sitting with the BBC director, Brian Hill. The rest of us just sat in pure amazement. Laurie returned to our table and demanded that the whole thing be aborted. He said they were paying $10,000, so we should just forget it. We had agreed that Laurie would be our spokesman, so we should all have taken this as being a definite no. Laurie had only to look at our faces, however, to know he was not the most popular person in the room, so we sat in a huddle and whispered our fors and againsts.

In the end Laurie relented, but this was totally against his better judgement. How can one man be right so many times? I can always count on Laurie's gut feelings, so why didn't we just stick with him on his first decision?

There was one other aspect to our decision though. We thought that if they showed the guys racing, or the racing car, we might get a sponsor, and yes, that idea had merit. Laurie was still very tight-lipped about the whole deal, but we had all decided to go ahead and so he went along with our decision. The verdict was that we would accept the challenge. Paul Watson said he would give us a little more time and would contact Laurie in the morning.

Joanne, Paul and Dione had already gone home, so this left Laurie, Mick, Yvette, Michael and myself walking up the street. We all said it would be okay, just another phase in our already complicated lives.

I knew that Joanne and I were going to have words when we got home. During the evening I'd whispered to Paul to tell her to take it easy with the wine, as she was getting pretty vocal, but I was not prepared for what awaited me when we did arrive at the house.

There, on the kitchen bench, was this little note:

*Mum*

> *I don't want to do this ABC thing and it's going to be impossible to live here while it's on, so I'm moving out for 6 months.*
> *Will call you tomorrow.*
> *Love Joanne*

I raced into her room and opened wardrobes and drawers, but it was true — the room was all but cleared out. I was hysterical. Laurie and Michael tried to comfort me, but Laurie was in tears. Why, why why? I had a very sleepless night: I walked into Joanne's room and just cried and cried. Laurie sat with me and we were both absolutely amazed by what had happened. She'd seemed to accept the whole idea as being a fun thing to do and had been quite okay about it until that night.

Joanne rang the next morning. I was full of emotion as this little voice told me not to worry, don't be upset and that she would be fine. All I could ask was: 'Where are you; where are you?' After 23 years of my worrying and working for her, she told me she had gone back to live with her father.

I couldn't believe it — it was like a clout across the ear. I sat on the bed and quietly pulled myself together and asked why, after all these years, had she gone back to her father? I received no help from him, no assistance with schooling and no presents for the kids, and Joanne had gone back! Of course, I never had exclusive rights to the children but I was so very hurt. I felt numb — as if a part of me had died, and I guess it had.

# The filming

## 6 December, 1991

T HE morning that Joanne rang was also the first day of filming, and it was a disaster. I was heartbroken over her sudden departure and the house was full of cameras, crew and excitement. On top of it all Paul had a go at Laurie, accusing him of being the reason for Joanne's departure. The whole thing got out of hand and we were being filmed, so Laurie went to Paul Watson and requested that they stop the camera. The request was granted, fortunately, but this is when we should have realised that we were in for some stormy times with this documentary.

Paul was completely out of line and some of the things he said to Laurie were so hurtful and hateful. But none of this commotion was going to bring back Joanne. (To my Joanne, from the bottom of my heart, I miss you and will always love you until the day I die.)

Everything was so different with the film crew in the house. We had people sitting around filming the cats and dogs eating — the normal things that happen each day. They filmed Laurie and myself arriving home from work, coming inside, opening the mail and being unhappy with the bills. Just the normal things.

We discovered that Mario the soundman and Paul the cameraman were the crew who had made *Cop It Sweet*, the controversial documentary about the police. We had many discussions about this — we asked questions and they told us what they had done. They explained that they hadn't been involved with the editing, so they felt excused from the backlash that hit after the show went to air.

\*     \*     \*

Now and then the crew would just sit in a room and not film, unless there was something of interest, or to keep themselves awake. In fact, Laurie kept asking them what their directions were, but the answers from the two BBC directors seemed to answer all our anxious questions. No, there would be no-one telling the story — just cold facts. What was said and done would be shown as it was.

During the filming the TV crew certainly fitted into our household very well. In hindsight, I think that they were instructed to do just that, not merely for the Donaher family's sake, but to make us forget that they were there. You must remember that the producers knew exactly what they wanted from the exercise, as they had done it once before in England and had experience from a similar TV documentary filmed in the USA. They certainly knew how to go about filming the right stuff.

As the time went on we all became quite used to having a microphone attached and we just went about as normally as we could. Of course we did tend to contact the next household if the crew said they were going there. If they were going to Mick and Yvette's, I would call Yvette and say that they were on their way, and she would do the same with me. It was quite exciting, although we felt that the footage they had taken in the first two to three weeks could not be of any interest to viewers. Paul and Dione were more interesting subjects, I guess. Dione was having her first child and coming to the end of her pregnancy. We all thought 'millions of women have babies every day', but the crew had already outlined what they wanted. They would just film anything and everything and show what they felt was the best footage.

Christmas was nearing and because everyone was feeling the effects of the recession we had decided not to have Christmas presents. We would have Christmas Day at our house, but with no presents (although Paul and Dione did bring some small gifts for us). I know that Kate, one of the BBC directors, thought this very strange, and so did I. Never again would I like to have Christmas Day without presents, but that was the way Christmas 1991 was.

# 24 December, 1991

Our business was down to minimum staff, so instead of taking our workers out to a restaurant or somewhere special that our bank balance wouldn't allow, we invited them to our factory for drinks and eats. We all pitched in and prepared the nibbles and it was just a very quiet afternoon drink. We were filmed socialising with our staff and workers, but I left early to do Christmas Eve preparations like stuff the turkey, make the trifles, etc.

The crew and cameras came home with me and filmed just that. It was repeated several times so the camera could pick up every detail. Mario the soundman made me a drink — my usual Jim Beam and Coke — and everything was normal that night. My sister came in after she'd finished work and she had a wine. We chatted about this and that, and yes it was Christmas, but neither my sister nor I was drunk.

We were asked to leave our front door open that night, as the crew wanted an early start and we were not to get out of bed until they had arrived. We did just what they asked and when they were in position we toddled downstairs. I fed our two cats and we sat having a cup of tea.

# 25 December, 1991

Early on Christmas Day in Sylvania Waters a few residents set out in their boats around the waterways with Christmas carols and good cheer. It's a lovely way to start Christmas Day and the little children love to see Santa aboard. From watching this we went inside with our neighbours and had a glass of champagne. Normal and uninteresting, but the filming went on. Laurie had bought a jet-bike (a two-seater aquatic motorbike) for the family for Christmas and Paul the cameraman went for a double with Laurie to film the water-ways. Being kind and generous, Laurie also suggested that Paul take it for a ride without the camera, but he got told off by the Water Police who patrol the area. The jet-bike was put away for the time being!

All the family arrived for Christmas lunch and we also had the pleasure of Joanne's company. She made it very clear, however, that if she was around not even a shadow of her frame was to be shown in the series. This was verbally agreed to by Paul Watson — her wish would be completely upheld. It was confirmed by all the crew — they knew that Joanne was not to be filmed *at all*. This they did not stick to, however.

Michael was in England with his school rugby team, so they had another crew filming him playing at Dulwich. When he rang home he was just furious. He felt the crew had tried to make a goose of him and his team mates. They even went into the shower rooms and filmed the boys half-naked. My word, he was very cranky, I can tell you. We felt a bit lost without him and I had a little weep, which was quite natural, when he rang. The camera zoomed in on me, but I later had the assurance that this segment would not be used.

# 26 December, 1991

On Boxing Day we took the boat up to Sydney Harbour to watch the start of the Sydney to Hobart yacht race. This is a magnificent day, with masses of boats gracing the harbour: a maze of sailing boats, small boats, large boats, ferries — every kind of craft. This is Sydney at its finest and the perfect occasion to show the people of Britain how beautiful our harbour is. They had a helicopter filming us coming into Sydney Heads. The pilot would zoom down, then up, and this went on for 10 minutes. The expense of filming must have been astronomical.

They filmed for hours and then we moored in the harbour and had lunch. A discussion started on older women having babies and the film crew went into full swing. After the lovely day we'd had we didn't care — perhaps they were bored out of their minds and just wanted something to do.

*　　*　　*

We went to Doyle's Restaurant one night and that was super too. Our meals were wonderful and I guess that was because the cameras were there. New Year's Eve was another beautiful night on the harbour and the fireworks were a pleasure to watch. We are so lucky in Australia.

The crew left us alone for the next week, to edit and have time out with their respective families, and we rather missed them.

# Second thoughts

RIGHT from Christmas Day, Laurie felt he knew what the crew were all about, and they had him worked out well too. Laurie would purposely go down and bury himself in the boat's engines, or climb under a car, to make it hard for them to film him. In fact, at times I thought he was very rude to them. Everything they wanted to do, somehow Laurie would do the opposite. He got stroppy when they wanted to go to the Motor Boat Club with all their gear and equipment in case they damaged the boat. For the $500 we were getting per week between three homes was it worth it? The directors were not very fond of Laurie, but he was certain that we were going to be very surprised by the outcome.

I had an in-depth conversation with Brian Hill, one of the BBC directors, about Laurie and the filming. Brian assured me not to worry and that half of what was filmed would be cut. Brian was frustrated by Laurie's behaviour and complained that he was making things impossible. I tried to explain this to Laurie on Christmas Day after the kids and crew had gone home. He still felt they were up to no good. He believed that they were filming controversial matter deliberately to promote the show, with no feelings for our family. Laurie had definitely formed his own conclusions and felt that the directors were jealous of our lifestyle, or of the way Laurie and I handled and controlled the rest of the family.

There were countless times when Kate or Brian from the BBC would contact me to say that Dione was being difficult and making it hard for them. Poor Dione was in the final stages of pregnancy so I understood the situation, but Kate was getting very upset with her.

The crew was at our home one evening when I was preparing dinner. Laurie came in from doing his odd jobs and went to get himself a beer, and me a bourbon and Coke. It was news time and Michael and I were discussing something too loudly, so Laurie turned the sound up. Mario the soundman turned it down and this continued and developed into an argument. Laurie said: 'Mate, if you want to film, then I'm sorry you will have to wait until the news is over, because at this time of day, this is what we do. We watch the news'.

Mario didn't like this at all and for a split second I thought Laurie was going to strike him. But Brian came on the scene and calmed them both down. We watch the Channel 9 news and Brian explained that they could hardly have this on an ABC documentary. After the scuffle the crew left for the night, but Laurie was still screaming about the whole incident.

Kate began setting up scenes, which might start with a question to keep the conversation going, like: 'What do you think should happen to the Australian flag?', or: 'Do you think there are too many Asians in Australia?' We knew when the crew wanted a break, as they'd put the camera on the pool table and wander outside. Whenever this happened you felt sure you weren't being filmed, but I made many regrettable misjudgements over this. I am the first to get into a discussion on how the country should be run.

We had been to Hong Kong and I was telling a story to the family, Kate and the crew. I had a whinge about a waiter who brought tea to our room one morning while Laurie was in the shower. I had answered the door and asked the waiter to place the tray on the table in our suite. He then took a few steps back and just looked at me. I hunted frantically for some spare change and even called out to Laurie, who didn't hear me. I explained to the young man that I didn't have any money and he certainly let me know he wasn't pleased — he all but spat at me.

This was one of those conversations that should be kept within the walls of your house, but we were such trusting little souls. The crew told us of similar incidents to my complaint and so it became a general conversation. I have met many lovely Asians, unlike that rude young man in the hotel, and was sure that what I had said was not going to be used against me.

On many occasions they would give us a leading question like: 'What do you think Paul and Dione would be best to do at this stage of their lives?' We would answer and later they would go to Paul and Dione and tell them what we had said, to get their reactions. I knew this was happening because we would discuss what was going on when they filmed at whoever's house that day.

Michael and I had been introduced to a dietary food, and for a little something to do we thought we would promote the product in our area. Michael was putting flyers into letterboxes and on cars at shopping centres and we were doing okay, with a growing clientele. The problem was that most of the ladies got such a fright to see a film crew in the house that we lost our clients. Firstly, they did not want to be on the show and perhaps they were also wary of outsiders knowing they were on diets. One woman called to make me promise that her mother would not be in the documentary.

The crew met us at the Motor Boat Club one Friday night and spent the evening filming Yvette and myself playing the poker machines. We played without hesitation and at the end of the night we all went for a Chinese dinner. Brian then asked Laurie to take his time going home as they wanted to film us arriving and had to get into position. We drove home, parked the car in the garage and Laurie and I thought of a little plan. We would go upstairs and change into something more comfortable, like they do in the movies.

I went up and changed and Laurie arranged the table on the upstairs balcony and poured us a port each. When I came out and sat down I discovered the cushion was full of water and I was soaking wet, but we performed in the spirit of things. While the cameras weren't rolling (or so we thought) Laurie had a discussion with the crew about black people. We were assured the cameras hadn't been in action, so we went off to bed.

We often asked the crew about the show and were always told it was coming along just fine and we would be pleased with the results. Little did we know what they were up to.

Yvette called me one day to say that she had discovered they'd filmed a segment on Laurie's ex-wife. I confronted Brian with this and asked why they would bring another side of the family into the documentary? He replied that it was getting a little boring and this would spice things up. I fell out of my tree and a heated argument started — Brian was very disgruntled with me that night. He later suggested that if he showed me this particular segment, would I then give the okay for it to be screened? I was adamant though, so he finally gave in and said that although they wanted to include it, he would grant my request.

After Dione had Kane in January I was a very proud and elated grandmother. Kane was so perfect — so much hair, big feet just like his father and grandmother, but so very, very perfect. A couple of times, when I visited Dione at the hospital, she was so upset. She complained bitterly about the crew and their constant filming. Her mother, who, with respect, wanted nothing to do with the show for reasons of her own, couldn't even visit in peace. In the end Paul got so upset one day that he asked them all to leave. I was amazed that the hospital staff had allowed this to be so constant, for I felt that Dione needed her rest. She was completely worn to a frazzle.

We had been asked to contact the crew each day to let them know what we had planned, or they would call us and enquire what we were doing. If it was of no interest they would leave you alone and go on to the next family. I go to the hairdresser's most Fridays and on one occasion the phone rang and the lady hairdresser was asked to stop washing my hair until the crew got there. Why would they want to film me having my hair done? I refused to be filmed with my hair being washed and when Kate and the crew arrived I was not a popular person. I really didn't care — I would like to think that me having my hair washed would *not* interest the Brits.

Dione rang me one day, furious and embarrassed. They had conned her into having her sister over for a girl-to-girl chat about sex. Dione should have turned this idea down, but thinking she was doing the right thing she allowed the filming to go on. I had never heard Dione talk about this subject and she assured me that she'd never previously had a discussion of this nature with her sister either. As you can see, the plot was in full swing by this stage.

# The promotional tape

B Y May, the five or so months of filming had been completed and in early July the ABC invited us all to watch the 20-minute tape that would be used for media and promotional purposes.

## July, 1992

When we all arrived at the ABC the gentleman on the gate knew we were coming and showed us where to park our vehicles. At this stage we were still one big happy family. We walked into the foyer — everyone knew us and called us by our first names — and we were taken into a boardroom to meet some of the hierarchy from Channel 2. Harry Bardwell, the ABC executive producer for the series, and Chris Pip were there and we had very nice nibbles and drinks and a wee chat. Then it was the time we had all been waiting for! Brian and Kate had told us it was fantastic and the public would love every one of us.

We were seated, feeling happy and joyful, and on went the promo tape. Promotional means to advertise, so to my knowledge this tape was what the media would see before the series was screened.

Most of the material was from the first show and there I was ranting and raving around the kitchen, arguing with Laurie. My darling Laurie must have seen the look on my face, for he reached out for my hand as a form of comfort. We suddenly realised it was Michael doing the voice-over. I was very proud of my littlest son — here he was telling the story so well, but we had no idea of what had been going on. The crew had been recording this voice-over in Michael's room throughout the five months of filming, without our knowledge. The problem was that Michael's commentary caused even more rifts in the family and if I'd known about this then, I would have stopped the series from going to air.

This promo tape practically threw me off my chair, but we coaxed the ABC into letting us see the tape of Dione and Paul's wedding. I loved it, absolutely loved it. All my fearful pea-brain thoughts of me screaming around the kitchen disappeared: perhaps they were all correct when they said it was going to be a great show. They gave us a fax from Paul Watson, reassuring us that all was okay and the show must go on. Big of him.

The ABC then gave us a list of potential managers, but my query was why, if this was just a documentary, would we be needing a manager?

We also asked about copies of the tapes for each of the 12 episodes. Our contract said that we would get these when the series was completed, but we were told that was not until after it had gone to air.

Paul was very definite about wanting a manager — there and then, that night. Laurie was against it, though, and I agreed. The whole show was just going to be boring.

At this stage the programme was not called *Sylvania Waters*; our surnames would never be used, nor our street name divulged. We trusted them to this extent and I comforted myself that everything would be okay.

# The publicity

THE first show was to go to air on 21 July, but the publicity started as early as a month before with an article in *The Australian* newspaper. The article described what the programme was all about and ended with: 'The Sylvania Waters family awaits ultimate exposure — probably more than they intended — on the media confessional.' It was a sign of what was to come.

## Sunday 12 July, 1992

Ron, our office manager, rang very early to say we should get the *Sunday Telegraph* and turn to page 38. Off Laurie went to get the papers and Michael and I joined him to read this full-page article on *Sylvania Waters*. It was subtitled: **MEET THE DONAHER FAMILY — REAL-LIFE PEOPLE WHO WILL STAR IN A REAL-LIFE SOAPIE**, and described the show very well. The

# SYLVANIA WATERS

## Meet the Donaher family — real - life people who will star in a real - life soapie

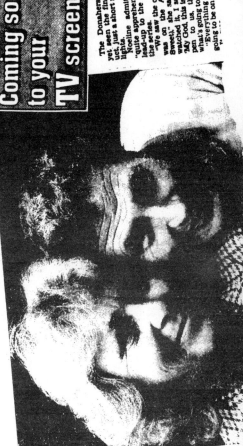

"FOR God's sake, he can have a bloody party," yells Noeline, her blood pressure rising as she storms around the kitchen.

Sitting at the breakfast bench, Laurie, her husband, is visibly enraged: "Of course he can, but he's just saying that if they're all going to bring friends and there's a million people here, we haven't got the room."

Son Michael, who is trying to plan his forthcoming 16th birthday party, shuffles his feet and gives the appearance of wanting to be anywhere but in the kitchen at this moment.

"Of course we haven't got the room," Noeline continues loudly. "He's not stupid!"

Laurie doesn't take a step back. "Well, you heard what he just said, Noeline."

Exasperated, Noeline, at the top of her voice, declares: "God strewth, Laurie, one of these days I'll pack me bloody bags and I'm going out of here — truly! There's more drama living in this house than living out of it!"

MEET the Donahers, of Sylvania Waters. It is perhaps not the best time to visit. Laurie and Noeline are midway through a do-

The Donahers have not yet seen the finished product, just a short reel of highlights.

Noeline admits to being "quite apprehensive" in the "quite apprehensive" in the lead-up to the premiere of the series.

"We saw the cop show that was on the ABC (Cop It Sweet)," she says. "After we watched it, I said to Laurie: 'My God, this is going to happen to us. This is exactly what's going to happen to us, we say is going to be on that box.'"

writer, Phil McLean, would have to be, in my estimation, the most caring journalist of all. He wrote the story pretty much as we had described it. This was one of only three interviews we had given since the filming began in December.

There was also a full-page article in the *Sun-Herald* on that day, headed **FAMILY BARES ALL FOR TV**.

We had been told there would be very little, if any, advertising, but open the *Woman's Day* and there we were; open *TV Week* and there was full-page advertising for the documentary. The *TV Week* advertisement had my sister, Annette, captioned as 'Pat the neighbour' and described the show as: 'An enthralling documentary series'.

# Saturday 18 July, 1992

Then came Richard Glover, of the *Sydney Morning Herald*, who wrote an article about us and one of the families who was shortlisted for the documentary.

He described us as: '. . . Australia's new ambassadors: a family whose members are variously materialistic, argumentative, uncultured, heavy drinking and acquisitive,' and then went on to compare us with the more 'artistic' Golski family. That was bad enough, but he then said, quite wrongly, that we supply non-union labour to the metal industry.

*Richard Glover, you have cost our business dearly with the nonsense you blatantly told the world about us supplying non-union labour to the metal industry. What would you know? What do you know of us? Laurie even went to a solicitor, but you still managed to say your piece on the front page. Where did you put your retraction three days later? Not on the front page. You will be pleased to hear that our business has suffered from that statement. Had you paid us the courtesy of meeting us, we could have explained how we operate.*

*Since that article I have met the Golski family. They are one-up on us: at least you went to their house for a ten-minute interview. Richard Glover, your lesson for the year should be to report the truth, not what you suppose to be the truth. You also spelt my name wrongly.*

To set the record straight, our company supplies contract labour to non-union factories, but when it is a union site we abide by the requirements one hundred per cent. Richard Glover's sensationalist remarks suggested that we do not follow the union's rules, and this has cost our company a lot of work. This is a great shame, for supplying labour to companies in the metal trade industry is all we know at our ages and the business he has cost us is irretrievable.

I think that we live in a free country and Laurie and I do believe in unions, but in our opinion they are too powerful and relentless. Perhaps with the country as it is today the unions should take heed and let us repair ourselves as a nation, while still having unions for the workers. That is my opinion, anyway, and I have spoken to so many companies and people who agree with me on this subject.

**PAUL**

*Sun, surf and a pregnant de facto. Life's dice don't seem to roll Paul's way – and at 26 he still can't cope with Laurie as "Dad."*

**MICHAEL**

*Noeline's youngest son. He's having a tough time of it lately – school pressures, Mum, Laurie, and puberty!*

# *Could these be your neighbours?*

**MICK**

*Laurie's junior petrol head, no worries. Loves his wife Yvette's body as much as his and dad's new race car.*

**DIONE**

*Dione loves Paul, but what she'd really love is a wedding. Money's tight so maybe after the baby is born.*

**YVETTE**

*Mick's wife isn't so keen on her own body and desperately wants to lose weight – or should she just have another baby?*

**PAT**

*The neighbour and Noeline's bar room confidant.*

**LAURIE**

*Boss Hog (or is he?) Laurie is a mature-age petrol head who loves his toys, and Noeline. Now their castle is built, they plan to marry after 13 years of de facto bliss.*

**NOELINE**

*Mum rules the roost – and the bar. As much as she tries to keep her "Brady Bunch" family in harmony, it isn't always so. She loves Laurie.*

# *Sylvania Waters*

### AN ENTHRALLING DOCUMENTARY SERIES

AN ABC-BBC CO-PRODUCTION

Ever wanted to know what the neighbours lives are *really* like? Ever wanted to be a fly on the wall in someone else's home? Well now you can, thanks to a brilliant new documentary series on ABC Television: *Sylvania Waters*. Over a five-month period, a small film crew was able to capture candidly the trials and tribulations of a real family. As you meet Laurie, Noeline and their family, you're not only invited into their homes, you will actually share their lives.

**ABC TV**
IT'S YOUR NETWORK

# PREMIERES TUESDAY 21 JULY 9·30PM

IKA/ABC412

We have had so many things written about us being *nouveau riche*, with our launch, *Blasé*, moored at the back door. For everyone's information, if Laurie and I did not have our business (and thanks to Richard Glover's remarks, our business is all but over), and if we didn't go to work every day and work damned hard, there is no way we could afford to live in this house, or have the luxury boat and cars. You see, when everyone is still in bed at 5.30 on Saturday mornings Laurie is up with the newspapers, buying this or that, to do up or sell, so our family can live in Sylvania Waters.

# Sunday 19 July, 1992

By the Sunday before the show went to air we had seen the previews being shown on Channel 2, and newspaper reports from all over Australia. Who was giving this information out to the newspapers? It was none other than the ABC — yes, the ABC. I believe that this information which is supplied to the media is called a press-pack. Laurie and I were becoming so uptight about the series that we rang Chris Pip and asked, in fact Laurie demanded, to see the 12 tapes. Before too long Harry Bardwell from the ABC was on the phone to Laurie but, even though Laurie was getting a little hot under the collar, he just refused to let us see them.

It was at this point that we definitely knew the show was not going to be what we had expected.

We were out on a limb and very vulnerable to all who saw fit to write these dreadful, monstrous things about myself and my family, whom I loved very dearly. It was me who had thought it was a great idea. I'd lost my daughter and had my husband and extended family feeling tense and very nervous. The pressure was so great that Paul and Laurie had words, and were locked in to the extent that Paul had been cautioned about staying away for the time being. Heavens, how much more could there be? But it didn't stop there. It just went on and on.

# Monday 20 July, 1992

On the Monday after the Richard Glover article was published, Laurie went to a solicitor and, after paying $720 for 15 minutes, faxes were sent to the ABC and the *Sydney Morning Herald*. The fax to the newspaper requested an immediate front page apology, while we expressed our concern over the matter to the ABC.

I came home from work early that afternoon as I had to take Michael's ski gear back to the hire outlet. We did that, dropped Michael's friend off at the station and then drove home. As I was putting up the garage door, Michael remarked that there were reporters coming across the road. I immediately thought this must be another one of his jokes, but no, it wasn't a joke. This was the start of 36 hours of sheer hell.

I was shaking, and Allan from next door fortunately came to my rescue. He asked them to

# REAL LIFE SOAP

A new series starting on the ABC this week looks at the "typical" Australian

# Family in soapie Waters

By RACHEL BROWN

Cameras capture real life in suburban Sylvania

# Calm waters or rough seas?

Sylvania Waters, a 12-part documentary

Outside their million-dollar home is

# Plenty of grit in this 'soap'

ould you be brave nough to

birthday party plans which been right out of

# Stormy waters

By MIRANDA DEVINE

leave us alone, but they are like a fever. They just
sat in the street waiting to pounce on anything
that moved.

# Tuesday 21 July, 1992

The next morning was no better. The first episode
was to be screened at 9.30 that night and there
were reporters outside the house and phone calls
coming into the office. You have no idea what
these reporters say to you — I will outline something of this later.

There was a full-page article in the *Daily
Telegraph-Mirror* on that day, headed **STORMY
WATERS** and saying that by 10 o'clock that night
we would be cringing and wondering why we
had got involved in the documentary.

That afternoon, Laurie left the office at approxi-
mately 2 pm and drove home to find reporters
everywhere and, later, a helicopter hovering over
our house — just like in the movies. We even
braved all this and went out the back, where
reporters were positioned in small boats on the
waterway. There were TV trucks and crews in
the street and around the corner. The whole place
was a mess, and mess is just not the word for it.

\*     \*     \*

At 5 pm a reporter knocked at the front door,
saying she had the first episode in her bag and
would I like to see it? How do you think I felt? I
was in tears and close to hysterical. I would have
loved to see the tape, but what good would have
come of it?

# Stormy waters

By MIRANDA DEVINE

BY 10 o'clock tonight the family of Noeline Baker and Laurie Donaher will probably be cringing in their pastel living room, wondering why on earth they participated in the ABC-BBC reality-TV documentary on their lives.

The rest of Australia will be cringing in sympathy, too, because there's something about the voyeurism of Sylvania Waters that fascinates and repulses at the same time. You feel you almost shouldn't be watching as this family unwittingly strips itself naked, emotionally.

Judging by the scenes of drinking, racism, jealousy and bickering in the first episode, the welcome mat outside their canal-front home soon will disappear.

Already, Noelene and Laurie have retreated behind the lace curtains on their red-and-blonde brick house on MacIntyre Crescent, refusing all interviews except, through their agent Brian Walsh, and then reportedly only for money.

Sightseers have even begun cruising up the narrow canal in their backyard, pointing and snickering at the family, says another neighbour, Ann Norwood.

"They're not going to be private for long," she says.

And that's before the first episode goes to air tonight at 9.30.

The Baker-Donahers and their neighbours have not been allowed to view the show before it is aired and, according to neighbour and close friend Trish Wick, they're "very apprehensive".

"It was done in fun," she says, puffing on a menthol cigarette at her front door.

"But I don't know if people are going to take it that way."

There were times when Noeline asked the camera crews to stop filming, says Trish who appears with her husband Alan in the show.

"The cameras were meant to be turned off but we weren't sure if they were or not. And after a while you forget that they're there at all. Six months is a long time."

Within the first few minutes of the show, the British producer Paul Watson – who has described family as "a dreadful, vicious institution; it's so arbitrary" – shows his hand.

This is not going to be a glossy portrait of the Australian good life. Rather, it shapes up to be a vicious pulldown of the nouveau riche – tailor-made for British audiences.

It begins with a fight. Noeline and Laurie are arguing in the eat-in kitchen about whether Michael should have a 16th birthday party.

"For Gawd's sakes. He can have a bloody birthday party."

storms Noelene.

"There's going to be a bloody million people here," retorts Laurie, sitting on a stool under a portrait of Elvis.

"Gawd, streuth, Laurie. One of these days I'll pack my bloody bags and I'm going out of here," she says.

As the camera pans over the possessions of the family – a million-dollar house with swimming pool and four-berth cruiser named Biase ("'cos that's the sort of people we are," says Noelene) a Mercedes and a four-wheel drive – Michael Baker, 16, narrates.

"I don't know if we're a typical Australian family but this is our life."

Noelene (who looks like Noelene Hogan and who is originally from New Zealand) introduces herself early on.

"I'm me. I can't be nice. I can't be Joan Collins. I'm me. I'm me."

Laurie's first words: "Driving a racing car is like going to bed with a good woman. Very exciting. Very exciting. Very exciting."

In real life, Sylvania Waters looks like the set of Neighbours – curving wide streets with double-storey houses, palm trees, garden gnomes and Spanish villa-style porticos. Every house seems to have a pool and musical door chimes.

The family includes Hoges-lookalike Paul, 26, and preg-

nant girlfriend Dione, who live in Mortdale. Paul works for Telecom and likes "going surfing and playing with my animals and Dione". Dione says "ohmigod and unreal".

There's Laurie's son Mick who's married to his childhood sweetheart Yvette and their two young daughters.

Tension comes from Paul who has never accepted Laurie, even though he moved in with Noelene 13 years ago.

Producer Watson, who specialises in candid camera portraits of families, says about Australia: "This is the land of opportunity. Let's look at people who have made their money. After achieving their dream, what happens."

None of the neighbours can understand why the Baker-Donahers agreed, reportedly just for expenses, to allow the cameras access to every inch of their lives for six months (barring the bedroom and bathroom).

Watson says the reason the family agreed is that "People who are ordinary – unlike politicians and journalists and celebrities who go on chat shows – are rarely asked for their view or asked to show their way of life and that's what gets people very interested in participating."

"They're very brave," says neighbor Rhonda McMaster.

"We're just looking forward to watching it. I think everyone in the street will be watching."

By 7 pm the media was everywhere. Channel 9's *A Current Affair* were next door at Allan and Pat's to film them watching the first show and the crew planned to come to our house at 10 pm to get our reactions. It was all too much, so we decided to get out and go to Mick and Yvette's to watch the first episode. What *was* all this fuss about? It seemed that everyone knew more about this show than we did.

We arrived at Mick and Yvette's, settled in and then there was Byron Hurst, a local Council member, on the television. He was standing on a pontoon in the waters, saying that this show *Sylvania Waters* was not, in his mind, good for the shire, etc, etc. Why would he be saying these things? Hell, what could be wrong? Before I left home that evening I had received a bunch of flowers and a bottle of champagne from the ABC, and here was this man carrying on about the show.

We had the ABC's *7.30 Report* to endure. They did a segment on *Sylvania Waters* and of all things we were introduced as Noeline and Laurie Donaher. Now, there were some conditions to be adhered to here! We had been told our surnames and addresses would be withheld, but here we were being named, and MacIntyre Crescent mentioned (another little slip?), *on an ABC current affairs programme, before the show had even gone to air!*

# The Episodes

I will now go through each episode with you and explain how the show went so very wrong. I am sure that anyone who has watched the entire series would draw the same conclusion that I have. It is quite one-eyed.

# EPISODE ONE

## Tuesday 21 July, 1992

THERE was Laurie, Mick, Yvette, my Michael, Lisa, Kristy and myself sitting at Mick and Yvette's waiting to see the first episode of *Sylvania Waters*. Why they had named it this, instead of 'The Family', was beyond me.

By the end of the first 10 minutes I wanted to run for cover. It was terrible. There was yelling, shouting, me prancing around the kitchen while we were arguing about Michael's forthcoming birthday party. Oh, Paul Watson, why did you have to take this line; why did you do this to us?

The music was great, the views were great and Michael's narrating was great as he introduced the family. Then it went straight on to Paul telling a story about how Laurie used to take the knobs out of the television when they were children. Now, let me tell you that the knobs were taken off because the kids were always fighting about what they wanted to watch. Laurie also wouldn't let the kids watch their programmes when we went out, which was never until it was near their bedtime anyway.

Paul said that Laurie used to hit him: I say again that I have never known Laurie to belt Paul to this day. I don't know how I can ever change Paul's mind about me having the business before I met Laurie, if this is something he believes. I worked for a company at Taren Point when I met Laurie and we built our business up together. Laurie did not, as Paul thinks, walk into my already-thriving business.

Then they showed Laurie and I haggling over biros. Well, you can't tell me this sort of thing doesn't happen in any average family.

On to my story about Hong Kong and the racist remarks about Asians. That was low of the crew and the repercussions could have been worse than they were. Oh yes, I said those things, but is it not so that what you say within your own four walls remains there? To me, they showed no regard for my questionable remarks, and I did not think for one minute that they would use them against me. Why did they show this? Okay, we might have been told we'd be filmed warts and all, but to deliberately set this up against me is, in my mind, quite evil.

They showed me talking about saving money and what you can have if you do. Then it was straight to the club and me playing a poker machine, back to the family room and me talking about saving again, then back to the club. Was this to give the viewers a false look at what we do, or to discredit us?

I still cannot work out what upset the media so much about this first episode that they could write such monstrosities about Laurie and myself?

To me:

| | |
|---|---|
| Dione is pregnant | normal |
| Mick's love for cars | normal |
| saving money | normal |
| Paul at work | normal |
| Mick and Yvette at work | normal |
| Paul surfing | normal |
| Kristy and Lisa being bathed | normal |

My remarks about Paul and Dione saving their money were not meant as criticism, but as advice.

Paul said that Laurie is not his father and that he has never seen him as a father-figure. Perhaps, if Paul had respected Laurie as a stepdad, he could have made life much easier for all of us.

Until the last five minutes of the show I did not have a bourbon in my hand. So where was my new-found drinking problem that everyone would soon be talking about?

*Anyone can see that they have edited and placed every controversial segment to suit themselves and left us carrying the can. Thankyou Paul Watson, Kate and Brian so very much. You are all back in England and the public over here are just about to stone me to death.*

\*   \*   \*

There were mixed reactions when the curtain fell. I was just disgusted with myself: I hated myself. Yvette was quiet and Laurie was disturbed, but

Michael was quite pleased with his effort. He had every right to be — he was easily the best part of the programme.

The phone was ringing hot at Yvette's. It rang and was answered — it was my sister Annette. Now that wasn't so bad. Then Yvette passed me the phone again — it was our manager, Brian Walsh. (We had decided that we did, after all, need a manager once the flood of publicity started.) His words were something like this: 'Don't be alarmed, but what I am going to say to you is very disturbing. I am sure that tomorrow they are going to publish an article about Laurie's past'. I tried to be composed, but was trembling and afraid he would not be able to get the article stopped. Brian said he would ring me back if there was bad news.

At this stage we were all making small talk: it was time for us to go. By the time we arrived home at roughly 11.30 pm the street was quiet. We fed the dogs, turned the lights off and went upstairs. Laurie and I discussed Brian Walsh's phone call. Laurie was in tears. 'Why would they want to destroy me?', were his words. He rang Allan next door and we sat in the kitchen with Allan and his wife Pat who, until now, knew very little about Laurie's past. Now all our clients would know too. What mayhem. Why, why, why? In the long run it would have been better if we had let this information be revealed, but here was my husband being threatened by my fantastic plan. What a disaster.

The information the press was about to release was going to destroy everything we had. It's probably a bit like war: you have to fight for what is yours. I had exposed the entire family to the media — be it radio, TV or the newspapers — and all we had built was about to be tossed around from radio station to TV news to the newspapers. I knew I had made a very bad mistake, but for how long do you have to pay? My god, you get less of a sentence for smuggling dope, or even murder.

Now we were over our first episode, but we were hurting and had done nothing more than to make a documentary series. I was already being called a racist, a drunk and a crass blonde and the next day was to be worse. My world came to a very abrupt end that night.

# Wednesday 22 July, 1992

I awoke after what seemed only a nap to find reporters at the front door. They must have been wanting blood, for they used every word uttered by us with venom. No mercy, no help. Nothing but: 'What is your reply to what Mr Such and Such said?' By this stage I was in shock and said something to defend myself, but I knew they would make it sound worse. What do you do? Change your name, change your hair colour, move house and then what?

Within two hours of my arriving at our office on that Wednesday our cleaning lady rang from the house to say that the front lawn was swarming with reporters, and what should she say? Our young man was mowing our lawns and the media

# Sylvania Waters a 'prison'

NOELINE Donaher, whose family is exposed in the reality documentary Sylvania Waters, was close to tears last night, a prisoner in her million-dollar canal-front home.

"I'm scared stiff," she said at her front door yesterday, hours before the first episode of the 12-part documentary went to air on the ABC.

The family argues openly on the documentary and talks candidly about sex.

"For something that started off as a bit of fun, it's blown up out of all proportion," Mrs Donaher told the Telegraph Mirror.

"I'm really frightened. After some of the things that have been said, I don't want to watch it."

Nor does Sutherland Shire councillor Byron Hurst, who said every-

By ANDREW STEVENSON and MIRANDA DEVINE

one in Sylvania Waters was holding "cringe plans to share the last harassment"

Mr Hurst blasted the program because it had portrayed the British audience "and the green welly brigade in Somerset will imagine we're a bunch of colonials."

"I have no problem—

this continues Continued Page 3

ABOVE: Noeline with Laurie . . . "I'm really frightened"   TOP: The setting for the show in Sylvania Waters

were attacking all aspects of our home. Allan from next door had to forcibly escort reporters from our back entrance — which you reach through two gates or from the water. You see, overnight we had become hot property. We had been made the worst spectacle of this century.

All I could say to our cleaning lady was to say nothing and they would go away. That was in my imagination: they would not go away. They asked immediate neighbours about us; they went to every local shopping centre just to get someone to say something about us. As far as our street went, most people did not even know our name. By day we go to work and at weekends we keep very much to ourselves, but the street was in uproar. Our children were bewildered and we could not believe what had happened.

Our solicitor, and a friend for many years, rang to tell us to turn the radio on, and we did just that. The talk-back shows were full of hate, sarcasm, hate, disbelief and more hate. Only the odd person said a little in our favour. And you call yourselves decent Australians! Heaven help us.

An article was published in the *Daily Telegraph-Mirror* on that Wednesday, quoting me as being 'scared stiff' and: '. . . close to tears last night, a prisoner in her million-dollar canal-front home'. Our home truly was becoming a prison.

\*     \*     \*

Things gradually got worse and worse. People didn't know whether to snub us or speak to us and it was just so damned horrid. We had kept to ourselves so much and now all of a sudden our tales were being aired by millions of people. Headlines in Sydney read: **STARS ONE DAY, GONE THE NEXT!** and **CRINGE! TV'S SYLVANIA WATERS COPS A LASHING**. This latter article said that 'cringe parties' were being held around the Sylvania Waters area because people were so embarrassed by us and the programme.

The newspaper articles just never stopped. Papers in Sydney, Melbourne, Perth and all the major cities and towns ran stories on the first episode and it was also reported that the ABC did well in the TV ratings.

Of course, the darlings from Britain had packed up their goods and gone safely home, assuring us that they would keep in touch. What a load of rubbish. I think the most humiliating aspect of the whole thing is that whenever I had spoken to Kate or Brian, not for one moment did they give me the impression that they had an inkling of what they personally had done to my life, not to mention my family's. I wondered silently what Paul and Dione, or Mick and Yvette, were saying in the quietness of their homes.

The first episode had left me drained, with a feeling of utter disappointment and contempt for the BBC. The 'warts and all' idea could have meant so many other things — yes, a tiff here and there, but racism? Heavens, Brian and Kate, I bet you were laughing all the way back to the cutting room and having a great time at my expense. If you ever feel pain, hurt and deception, I can tell you this is how you have left me feeling — as if my whole world has collapsed.

So many things were going through my mind about what could have been used, but after this first show I knew it would only get worse for all concerned.

\*     \*     \*

Yes, we had made a contract with the ABC and BBC to do a documentary on the everyday life of an average Australian family, but we went into it in complete innocence. We were thrilled and proud and felt privileged to be the chosen family. Never did we, in our wildest dreams, imagine the repercussions would be like this.

Did anyone who phoned the radio stations and described the show so cruelly on that Wednesday feel proud of what they said?

My children were involved in this turmoil and I had family in New Zealand whom I love very much, and who were also going to be hurt by the series.

But you see, there were 11 more of these programmes to get through and I knew it would be the death of me. That Wednesday was already the point of no return. In the end I rang Brian Walsh's office with a cry of: 'I need help!', and we had security men sent to the office and the house.

Is this what the ABC, BBC, media and reporters had in mind. Had they no sympathy for us? And so the reviews went on, the crippling remarks went on, and I thought you must all have been enjoying the situation. By then everyone with nothing better to do was getting on the bandwagon. Did it make you all feel better?

Channel 2 got a 20 in the ratings for the first episode and they thought it was fantastic. They, of course, did not really care about the abortion of our agreement.

Perhaps the majority of you are thinking that I knew what I was getting myself into, but you are wrong. I was quoted in the *Daily Telegraph-Mirror* on 22 July as saying that something that had started out as fun had been blown out of all proportion. I had no idea what to expect next and there were 11 more nightmares to go.

# EPISODE TWO

## Tuesday 28 July, 1992

BY the time episode two came round I had, of course, spoken to everyone in the family and we all drew the same conclusion: the first episode had been a shock. I had to wonder if I had been a character from one of the soaps, would I have received all this criticism? Things had been written about my family that I could not believe. They weren't content with screwing up my life, but had now gone to Laurie's first wife. They had asked in the local shops about me, they asked people in the street — all to sell their papers.

Take our local paper, the *St George Leader*, on Thursday 23 July. They reported that we have an Asian gardener and quoted a lady who later wrote me the following letter.

*Dear Mr & Mrs Donaher and family*
    *On Thursday, the* Leader *printed an article in which I was quoted. I would like to apologise for the comments that were printed, they were not*

*meant to be personal, or to hurt you or your family.*
*The paper printed only some of the comments —*
*and those out of context.*

   *I hope you'll accept this apology.*

I don't have an Asian gardener and what I was
saying about Asians in the first episode is that
this country is at its wits' end, so any person
living here who is feasting off our generosity
should go back to their own country to give us
some relief. Australia, in my estimation, is too
kind to all — not just Asians. We bring them in,
then we support them. No-one supported me
when I moved here from New Zealand.

   I must tell you that on the night of the first
episode the neighbours in our street were questioned. The report covered 15 homes and there
was only one negative: all the others thought we
had done a good job.

   The second episode started with all the empha-
sis on Paul versus Laurie, and Paul and Dione.
What infuriated me was that our friendly directors
had again directed their questions, and edited to
get just the replies they required to stir up the
public and make the situation between Paul and
Laurie even worse.

   I liked most of the scenes that were shown in
this programme. They got away from the bickering of the first episode, and showed a little of
the way we live away from the house with some
of our friends (who, by the way, supported us
through and after each episode).

   We did have a lovely Christmas and every
member of the family was very happy. Michael

was overseas, but he rang to speak to us all. Please think of how many rifts or altercations you have had in your household in the last six months. I have now witnessed two or three in our family in the first two episodes. It doesn't matter whether you live in Rotorua, New Zealand or Turramurra, Sydney, Christmas Day is a lovely day to spend with family and friends. I am not trying to score any points, but our Christmas Day would have been much the same as in your house.

By now the papers had branded me as having a drinking problem. Remember that the crew came to our house most afternoons at about 4 pm, and I do have a drink with Laurie before dinner. So the conclusion to everyone is that I have a drinking problem. Very unfair.

In this second show we were still having the same sort of discussion as the week before — mostly me yelling, to be correct. Please be aware that my son Paul is as much loved as any other member of our family, but I think Paul and I must have trusted the crew more, and when asked a question we told all. Stupid. Not one of us fully realised that this sort of footage would be of interest to viewers, but we did make a dreadful mistake, didn't we?

It was sad that they didn't show more of the Sydney to Hobart race on Boxing Day, for this is one of the highlights of the year for me. All we got was 30 seconds and then we were into the rowdy debate that I mentioned earlier about middle-aged people having babies. You see, once again they were not there for the scenery. They had already plotted what they intended to do.

No wonder the public was irate. There we were in the middle of a recession, and all we saw on this show was money, money, money! But we don't have a lot of money. We gave my godson, Jay, a truck for Christmas and it cost $45 on special, so I do watch my pennies.

Everyone in Australia presumes we are rich, however, with this million-dollar home on the water and a huge cruiser at the back door. And we drive expensive cars. By now I was branded as the Crass, Drunken, Loudmouthed, Screaming Woman. You only had to pick up any paper to see that is what the majority were calling me. We all know I am just a lanky kid from Inglewood, New Zealand, with big feet — not a big mouth.

*        *        *

At this stage I was finding it harder to cope with the press and media than the five months of filming. I was never quite a prisoner in my home, yet for four weeks I did no shopping. To go shopping meant that people would just stare and remember that the public, especially in my area, were livid by then. I thought we might be asked to leave the district, for they seemed to be ashamed of us. I was too.

The newspapers were really getting in on the act with headlines like: **'CRINGE PARTIES' BIG NOW IN SYLVANIA WATERS**, **DALLAS IN SUBURBIA: IT MAKES GROSS TV** and **IT'S LIFE, BUT IS IT ENTERTAINING?** One paper said: 'the Donaher family . . . sailed a fighting, bitching, well-heeled course over the horizon of their richly furbished Sylvania Waters home and into the loungerooms of those average Australians

who don't have pots of money'. Another said that
the programme should be screened in as many
countries as possible, as it would put people off
emigrating to Australia.

Oh boy, did I want to retaliate against these
monstrous allegations, but Laurie advised me that
this would only add fuel to the already blazing
fire. Those radio presenters sat behind their micro-
phones and just talked and fired more sarcasm at
me. All people had to do was to change to another
channel on Tuesday nights and they would have
been okay.

*Backchat* (the ABC's viewer-response show) was
by now cashing in on us too. Considering we did
this whole thing for the ABC, you would have
thought they could read out at least one good
letter. Oh no, we couldn't be that lucky. The word
cringe kept coming up: another of those choice
words. We were not cringing — we weren't coping
at all well, but I would not have called it cringing.

The ABC were doing alright out of it too. The
TV rating had been 20 after the first show and
Episode Two was still high enough to beat a couple
of other stations. One headline said: **WATERS'
KEEPS ABC AFLOAT**.

We had, though, received one positive fax, sent
to Mick and Yvette's workplace, from a family at
Avoca Beach, NSW. They had a very good attitude
and commended us.

*Dear Mick & Yvette & Family*
*Sorry to bother you at work but just a short
note to let you know how much we enjoyed the
show. Please let Laurie, Noeline, Paul and Dione
know.*

*The family's refreshing honesty was a joy to watch. Also please let Noeline know that there is hope for Dione and Paul. We were (probably still are) very similar to them with our surfing and love of animals but once our son Dane (2 yrs) arrived things changed. We now have bought a house and both have jobs in which we work hard.*

*Your family is so similar to ours with your open frank honesty. We feel we already know you and want you to know that you have our support and friendship.*

*Good luck for the future and don't let the bastards and knockers get you down.*

There were also a couple of favourable items in the *Sydney Morning Herald* — a letter, plus a review of the programme. Both of these defended us and the show, and said that much of the criticism was due to snobbery, and the fact that everyone is too concerned with what the British think of us.

\* \* \*

By now, our street was full of curious onlookers, so it became difficult to even go out to wash the car. Watering the plants was a problem too, for the canal was ablaze with more curious sightseers.

So what could we do? We stayed inside.

# EPISODE THREE

## Tuesday 4 August, 1992

A week later we seated ourselves for the third show. *Backchat* was on at 9.20 pm and our programme at 9.30 pm, so we always watched this first. Good gracious, they were *still* not showing one good remark, yet more and more people had stopped us in the street to say they'd written to the ABC. It appeared that there were more people liking the show than not. To keep the flame burning, the ABC obviously thought it was in their interests to read out only the worst letters.

The third episode began with Paul being pulled down the street on his skateboard by his dog, Bear. Great for me, especially, as I love to see my kids on the television. We then went straight on to Michael's narrating, telling everyone about how money is scarce, but that we have bought a racing car. We didn't have to fork out a lot of cash for it, as we had sold our previous Group A car and we certainly don't spend money willy-nilly. If we can't afford to go racing, we don't go.

The car racing scenes make the show more attractive and for me this is good viewing. Car racing has been our passion for a long time, and although Laurie and Mick are not rev-heads, they love the sport. Our Group A car is a joint venture and to set the record straight, Mick has paid his half of the car. I feel sure the directors told Paul that Laurie and I had bought the car, but that is not the case.

Mick then described how he met Yvette, and how upsetting it was to him when his parents' marriage came to an end. I wonder how much prompting the crew gave him. Fortunately for all concerned he only said what he had to say.

Michael's dreadful school report came while he was overseas with the rugby tour. We knew this scene would be used, and were very conscious of what to say and when to say it, but how many viewers have gone to the mailbox and been devastated by their child's school report? Was my bad reaction so different from yours? Education is so vital in this day and age.

Now to the bedroom scene. They did this to Mick and Yvette as well and I couldn't really see the point of including it in the show. It wasn't much fun having a film crew standing in our bedroom at 6.30 am, but now you have all witnessed Laurie and myself waking up. I wondered when they would show Mick and Yvette?

The best part of this show was my baby (Michael) coming home from his rugby tour — the best present I could have had. Michael had been so brassed off with the English crew filming his rugby match that he made me promise I would not allow the crew to be at the airport. They insisted on being there though, and Laurie and I relented only on the condition that they stayed right in the background. They did just that. Michael described me as: 'She's just Mum'. So you see he missed me too — I don't spend every waking hour screaming at him! Then we had the nice homecoming party for Michael.

It was then on to Paul and Dione's house. Dione was telling everyone how her parents and in-laws to-be were interfering with names and suggestions for the baby. For the life of me, I don't recall suggesting any names but there we were hearing all this on television.

On to the subject of Michael's long and dirty hair. I make no excuses here, for I am very old-fashioned. I like boys or men to have short hair and I don't like earrings for men, but that is only my opinion.

Now the 'washing the hair' segment. It was a free-for-all that day: the crew said something like: 'Let's have a little fun; make Michael wash his hair,' and in the spirit of the moment Michael and I did just that. But who was really interested in Michael washing his hair? The crew again said that they were only filming something to keep themselves awake.

No wonder Yvette was getting more and more paranoid about what she had seen so far. They could have shown so many beautiful segments on her, but there she was discussing her weight problem in front of millions of people. I bet she was only sitting and talking generally with the director. She is a very sensitive girl, and to have this flashed across the screen was so embarrassing. How dare they use this as part of their little show! Yvette, like me, was going out less and less to do her shopping.

You have to remember that we had watched nothing other than the 20-minute promotional tape and the film of the wedding. Just like all of you viewers, we were seeing this for the first time. They were beginning to trip themselves up at this stage though, for we purchased the racing car earlier but then they showed Mick on the telephone talking to Laurie about selling a few things to come up with his half of the money.

We knew that the crew spent a great deal of time with Paul and Dione, but this seemed quite understandable as Dione was having the baby. I had to wonder, though, why they kept comparing our standards of living? They'd zoom in on our house from the street, then to Paul and Dione's home. Then there were the scenes where other members of the family were enjoying themselves in some way or another and generally spending money, and Paul and Dione were broke. This happened too many times to be coincidental. These are controversial matters that helped to create the publicity, but with no regard as to what it would do to the family.

*       *       *

We had letters after this show telling, or should I say advising, Michael to pack up his bags and leave home before we destroyed him. You must understand that our house is for all to enjoy. I don't have a husband who goes to the pub every day, and I must say he is an excellent husband. He loves his home and likes to have his family and friends around for an Aussie barbecue and a drink and game of pool.

My personal view is that I didn't think the show would attract this much attention, and I don't think the ABC did either. We were told that the ratings had been up around 17, which they said was very good considering the Olympic Games were on.

It was becoming very hard to do our shopping as everyone recognised Laurie and I when we went out — it was very embarrassing. People did not believe that we had not received a lot of money to do the series.

Because I always answered the crew's questions I guess I could understand why the newspapers were out to get me, but it was like being tortured very, very slowly. Even our house, the only place where I could find peace, wasn't safe. Imagine being woken in the early hours of the morning by young people screaming out 'Laurie and Noe-line' as they drove past.

By now the uproar had subsided to quite a degree and, although we still had the eye-contact problem with people, we had to go out. We chose not to go anywhere on Friday nights though. Yes, we were still embarrassed and very unhappy with what the ABC and BBC had done to our family.

After the third episode Laurie made up his mind not to watch any more.

*     *     *

At some time in August I received a telephone call from Chris Pip of the ABC. She'd had a letter from Kathy Golski, from the family that was not chosen to do the documentary. Kathy wanted to paint my portrait. I can't describe what I felt — was I happy, or what?

> *Dear Chris*
>
> *I watched* Sylvania Waters *last night — we all watched it and decided that you have struck gold with Noeline. She is a wonderful foil for the whole domestic drama and in her own way has great stage presence (I would* not *be a match). Congratulations, really, on the whole thing, it is bloody good, and I for one am glad not to be in Noeline's position notwithstanding everything. Ask her if she'd like to have her portrait painted!*

So what was I to make of this? Did the Golskis just want to meet us and have a go at us, or were they genuine?

# EPISODE FOUR

## Tuesday 11 August, 1992

NOTHING much had changed on *Backchat*. There was one possibly good letter, but the rest really slammed us.

Episode Four centred around Dione's greatest moment — she was finally having her baby. Yes, they let the cameras in, but they were not to film while she was in the last stages of labour. Dione was quite upset with them all by this time and it's not everyone who would let a film crew do what she and Paul did. The cameras zoomed in on Paul, who'd had a torrid 24 hours and was obviously nervous. He was about to have a taste of fatherhood!

This episode was all over the place, though. We were on to me, dusting down the bedhead in the bedroom. I must have done this a thousand times — repeating the way I held the duster, etc, etc. I was casually talking about Paul: nothing dramatic. Then it was back to the hospital to see Kane being cleaned up. Now to me at the hairdresser's, of all places. In the background you could hear Dione fretting and there was I at the hairdresser's! Then back to Paul and Dione and their elation at their new pride and joy, Kane.

They switched back to Laurie and myself discussing how if Paul and Dione don't have a little more respect for money and budgeting, they are going to have a hard time making it. This was in January, the same month as Kane's birth.

On to Lisa's third birthday party, which was in February. If only they had screened more of the party and the fun the little ones were having. But no, they had to show Mick's mother, with Mick explaining that . . . 'this is my real mother and Noeline is my stepmother,' and this, that and the other thing. That was a juicy little part for Mick, but they then went back in time to January and to Paul and Dione bringing Kane home.

Then it was back to the discussion on Michael's appearance and attitude. Paul, Dione and myself were sitting outside at the hospital, having a cigarette and they were agreeing with me about what we should do with Michael.

More controversial footage: this was about the amount of $45,000 that Mick and Laurie were going to pay for the racing car. The camera zoomed in on Laurie writing the amount down on his desk pad. We then crossed to Dione looking through the paper and wishing she could buy a fridge and a playpen, then it was on to Mick talking about spending money.

They showed the outside of Paul and Dione's rented house *yet* again in this episode. When I was their age with my first child, Paul, I lived in less than that but made the best of it. My parents' house was relatively big and grand, but I never felt that they should give all this up to help me.

Paul and Michael were both mouthing off about Laurie, but didn't you hear Michael say that Laurie never hits him? No, he never has. My children are lacking one ingredient in that they have been brought up to respect their elders, but they don't.

Michael was being scolded in this segment over his general behaviour and the $100 bet he had with Pat from next door on the sex of Paul and Dione's baby. How was he going to pay off the debt if he'd lost? I feel that what Laurie and I were saying was correct. I had a tear in my eye when Michael went up to his room and had a little cry. I am no different from any mother — I hate to see my children upset and crying. (Could I have spoilt my kids a little too much?)

What an awful episode! I knew I would receive a lashing from the reporters and that the letters would come in thick and fast. Oh yes!

# Wednesday 12 August, 1992

So the fourth episode was over, but things were tense on Wednesday at the office. The prank phone calls were constant. I'd answer the phone to have no-one on the other end, or just the clunk of the receiver being put down. Reporters were ringing to give us an update, or ask what our reactions were and that sort of nonsense.

Then I heard Laurie on the phone, obviously to a reporter, trying to defend himself. Hell, this was the opposite of what he had drummed into me.

He kept saying: 'Don't make any comment and they will go away'. Well, it didn't go away, and neither did the article on Laurie in the *Truth*. I immediately rang the publicity lady at the ABC (who I won't name, but she was the only ABC person who could see how the programme was affecting us). She called her friend at the *Truth* and we were assured that the story was going to be light-hearted and of a humorous nature.

This, however, is what appeared on Saturday 22 August.

### LAURIE ASSAULT CHARGE

How very cute. We are (or should I say were) quite respected in our business, and here was a story on how Laurie rammed a hose down a man's throat, because this man was spitting on his children. Perhaps we would all have done a similar thing if it had been our children, but this was hot news. In a way, it had been burning a hole in the hands of the leading Sydney newspapers right from the word go.

# Sunday 16 August, 1992

On the Sunday after the fourth show Laurie asked Michael and myself to go to the football, assuring me that people from other suburbs would not even recognise us. I was sick of staying indoors, so it seemed like a good idea — this was turning into quite a normal Sunday! Before we left the house, however, Yvette rang to tell us to buy the *Sunday Telegraph* and turn to page 4. The corner shop was out of copies, due to a dispute of some

# LAURIE ASSAULT CHARGE

## Real real-life Sylvania drama

LAURIE Donaher, the dad in Australia's real-life Sylvania Waters soap opera, smashed a neighbor's teeth when he shoved a hose down his throat.

Donaher, who was convicted of assault and fined in a Sydney court after the incident, claimed the man had spat on his children.

The 46-year-old father of two, who has become a national television star since the ABC series about his family began screening five weeks ago, described the conviction and fine as a "travesty of justice".

● CONTINUED PAGE 2

★ NOELINE, Michael and Laurie Donaher . . . TV sensation.

sort at the newspaper, so it was not until we arrived at the sports ground that we got a copy. I turned to page 4, imagining that Laurie and I were being taken to task for upsetting Michael in the last episode, but there was the full-page story, with pictures, and the headline: **SYLVANIA WATERS ... THE STORY CONTINUES. DONAHERS STILL MAKE THE NEIGH-BOURS BLUSH.**

My entire body was screaming as I read on. Oh, heavens, they described our wealth, our mansion, our million-dollar waterfront home (I would love to see us get a million dollars for it at present). There I was again described as Noeline, the Brassy Bottle-Blonde, who watches all the soap-operas. For the record, I don't watch this sort of stuff. Laurie and I did watch a few episodes of *Chances* but it became a little over the top, and when you have to get up at 6 am each day there isn't much time for watching television.

This unnamed reporter's story was as accurate as the facts the ABC Publicity Department were giving out, and it was a load of rubbish. The article even told people what would happen in the fourth episode — two-thirds of the page described the following week's show, which of course we hadn't even seen.

Oh hell, this little amused person was going to write an article every week. Why hadn't we been advised that the publicity was going to be so hard and fast? We had been told not to expect great things from the show, but all this information was coming from the ABC Publicity Department.

*Thank you, reporter or journalist, for not letting me know your name. Did you feel comfortable writing this report? Did you ever consider how much anguish and heartbreak had already been caused. Boy oh boy, did you help me come closer to a nervous breakdown.*

You can imagine how, if I could have got my hands on one of the producers or directors, I think I could've committed murder. This was sheer hell, and for what — $13,999. (I should explain here that the original fee of $10,000 was later increased to this amount.) My goodness, how could I have been so blind. Laurie had the right idea that night we went for dinner with the crew: just forget it. I had involved so many of my family, thinking that this was going to be so much fun. How do I say I am sorry for what I have done to you all?

*            *            *

Harry Bardwell from the ABC has since told me that there were two letters (one was quite threatening) saying that if the show went to air, the author would spill the beans on Laurie. There we were, half-way through our lives, and still playing games — but with big people now.

By the time this book goes to press I am quite sure our business will be closed, thanks to all the publicity that has centred around Laurie and myself. This is all proving too much for our clients, who know that we live in this million-dollar house, although it's no mansion. I guess it is a case of envy rearing its ugly head. I hope you may understand my bitterness and the hurt that we have endured in the last few months of our lives.

The media have opened up some old wounds. The point is, you selfless little reporters, that Yvette and my children didn't know about all this, while our friends knew only a little.

The lesson is: never ring up for a competition of any description and never, ever, let a film crew do a documentary on you. Being a public figure was completely draining my mind and body.

The Donaher family with our entry in the Tooheys 1000 at Bathurst.
Left to right: Noeline, Laurie, Mick and Yvette

Noeline and Elizabeth Hayes serve lunch for the Wayside Chapel at the Hard Rock Cafe

Paul Baker (Noeline's son) with his son, Kane

Noeline and Laurie 'Signing our lives away'

Noeline and Laurie at the helm. 'The day we bought our second boat, 41 Ft Randell'

Mick Donaher—Laurie's eldest son—with wife Yvette and kids,
Kristy and Lisa

Noeline and Laurie hold the letter from deputy Prime Minister Brian Howe apologising for his description of Noeline which she considered inappropriate—Pictured at their Sylvania Waters home

Noeline and Laurie watch the final episode of Sylvania Waters

Noeline contemplates what the TV series has done to her life

# EPISODE FIVE

## Tuesday 18 August, 1992

ON to the fifth episode. Boy, were our little friends making life hard for us and showing Laurie and I at our worst.

This show started with Laurie and I cleaning up our old Buick, with the idea of selling it to make some money. We have been carrying quite a heavy financial burden for a couple of years, as the recession has been other than kind to us — it often amazes me how we have held on for so long. Anyway, the time has perhaps come for us to sell off a few of our assets and cut back on our motor racing. Much as I love the racing, it is just not worth the risk of losing my home and business. We have tried so hard to find a sponsor, but have had no success.

Incidentally, the series often mentioned us wanting to sell some of our possessions. In my opinion, though, you can't just up and sell things and lose money in the process. Brian Hill always seemed to be sneering at us, and Laurie felt this more than I did. On this particular day when we were tidying up the Buick, Brian was having a chat with Laurie. Quick as a wink, Brian asked: 'Why, Laurie, you can't be hard up and if you are telling the truth, why don't you sell the Buick?' Laurie always put it down to envy on Brian's behalf.

To go motor racing at Laurie's age you have to have a medical every year. This year Laurie was stressed out and found he was overweight and had high blood pressure when he visited the doctor. Laurie goes on a diet two days before he races, but it should be said that he loves a beer or two, just like any average Aussie.

For Laurie's sake, the doctor denied him a clean bill of health and he came back to the office very despondent. The doctor had also been shocked by Laurie's eight or nine beers each day, and up to 15 at weekends, and told him this had to stop. With the help of our crazy neighbour, Allan, we planned how to get Laurie back on the road to good health.

Although Laurie was going to be strong and give up his beer of a night, by the time 5 pm came round that day he relented about having a drink. On this particular day I made him a scotch and water. This wasn't right, so we tried scotch and soda, but that didn't suit him either. He was now desperate for a beer and the camera zoomed in on all the bottles on the bar. Let me enlighten you though, and say that most of this alcohol had been brought over by our guests for get-togethers and just left there. Our liquor stock has grown considerably in this way.

Now to Michael's school uniform. Michael didn't want me to escort him into the city to buy this.

I guess he may have had a little lady he wanted to see, and Mum he did not need. But who in their right minds would give a young guy, Michael in this case, $300 to take into the city to spend?

Michael can be a little brat and he has too much to say. You know, young people are all the same. When they are getting their own way things are just fine, but when you say 'no' you become a dragon.

In the next shot there was Paul in our backyard, looking happy and not screwed up for once. The problem with Paul was that the producers would ask loaded questions and, being gullible, he would respond just as they wanted him to.

Michael's voice-over explained the plot for Laurie to get a medical pass. I came up with the idea of giving him Phenergan tablets to quieten him down before he went to another doctor for an examination. I use only the 10 mg tablets, but Laurie went off and bought the heaviest dose and took two — by the time I had driven him to the surgery he was really woozy. He was all but asleep beside me and slurring his words! This second doctor passed Laurie though, saying his blood pressure was fine but that he must try his hardest to lose a couple of kilos.

Then it was on to me cooking rissoles. I don't know how many times they filmed me making dinner and I used to get very nervous having the camera 'looking over my shoulder'. I can tell you that my poor family had some very off meals during this period! The rissoles that night were no exception — they may have tasted okay but they looked dreadful. Laurie was still hazy from the Phenergan and you all saw him nearly pouring his beer over them instead of the tomato sauce. The Sunday papers really gave me a serve over that one!

Anyway, the whole of Australia saw how devious we all were. Here we had Laurie faking his medical (we fully realise that next year he had better lose those kilos and have his blood pressure A-Okay) and me making him scotch and soda and feeding him those awful rissoles. Lots of laughs for all of you and another tick for the BBC.

Over to Paul and Dione's, where Paul was holding little Kane and saying he liked being a father. I thought that was great.

You must understand here that the editing had been so precise that I was amazed any of us were still together by this stage. We had Laurie going off about Mick — there had to be better scenes they could have used. Then there was Paul and Dione sitting on a fence discussing me. The director must have told them about the conversation I had with him about them saving money.

Once again, we were all up at Eastern Creek Raceway, racing our new car and then we bounced over to have a look at Paul's car, which had a blown head gasket and there was no money to fix it. Paul chose to work for Telecom and go to work every day — so be it. Mick chose to be a mechanic and with his drive has set himself up with Ultra Tune, with all the headaches and heartaches that go with having a business. I would guess that Mick and Yvette don't take home the money that Paul does each week.

Directors Kate and Brian were still intent on

showing our home, then crossing to Paul and Dione's abode. There was us with money to buy a racing car and they had no cash to fix their head gasket. By now the whole thing was pulling at everyone's heartstrings. Laurie was upset with Paul for bagging him out all the time and I was in the middle, trying to calm the household.

How was I meant to control this upset, and why did the story have to go along these lines if it was only supposed to be a documentary?

*    *    *

I noted in my diary about a little chat I had with Brian during the filming as to how the show was coming along. He said it was going really well, but that Laurie would become the 'mongrel'. 'Why my Laurie?' was my first thought, but all Brian had to say was that someone has to be the mongrel in any story. Had I shown any regard for all concerned and told Laurie that day, I am sure we could have broken our contract then and gone on our merry way.

Some time later, when I did talk to Laurie, he just brushed the whole thing aside by saying: 'I'm always the mongrel around here', and, quite peeved, he stormed off.

# EPISODE SIX

## Tuesday 25 August, 1992

I had a few giggles over the sixth episode and found myself quite involved with it. But I guess the whole family had acquired acting skills by that stage of the filming.

By now my opinion was that we had been slaughtered in every way possible. In this episode they got Dione to have a discussion with her sister about sex and I felt we had been chosen, as an innocent family, to do a soap series without the actors. We will make spectacles of ourselves to the British audience. Thanks again, Brian and Kate.

Laurie and Paul were not even talking by the time this episode was screened and my life was unbearable. There was Laurie, looking in from the outside. You can bet his assumption was correct when he said very earnestly that my children speak to me as though I am a mound of dirt. We are not just talking about Paul here, but all three of my children. Instead of being second in charge of my home I must once again come sixth in line

— just like that little kid from Inglewood, New Zealand.

This episode started off at Paul and Dione's house, just so that everyone could see how poor they are — yet again. Dione was talking about her sex life since the birth of the baby, then they showed Paul speaking on the same subject. These controversial pieces were set up and were yet more examples of their fine editing. At this point the entire family was shuddering. Sure, we said all those things, but the 'befores' and 'afters' had been taken out and all the viewers heard were the juicy bits of each conversation.

Laurie was explaining a bit about our life and I think his intentions here were to say: 'Look, this is our life and the way we live it. We work for what we have and we enjoy it'.

I have already mentioned that Michael and I were selling a diet product in the area. It is a good product that helps you to lose weight, and I speak from experience here. This was how my girls' party came about.

Believe it or not, this was about the fourth such party in my life. To spice the day up, and get a good showing of heads, I thought of hiring a male stripper through the Yellow Pages phone book. When I explained what I required to the lady at the stripper company, she offered her husband. We had what you could call a funny conversation discussing how far he would strip and I made all the arrangements with her.

My idea made the girls come along and it was great fun, even if we didn't sell much in the way of products. Okay, so not many of the girls told their husbands or whatever about the stripper, although I feel sure now that the BBC directors had informed Laurie and, as you saw on the show, I told him about it afterwards.

The gentleman (and I'd like to make it clear that he was a complete gentleman in every sense of the word) who came to the house on the day of the diet party was the most magnificent specimen of a man most of us girls had seen. He was a gorgeous, massive negro with a smile that would charm my grandmother, if she were alive. The crew explained to our guest, Jean, that they would be filming and without further ado the party sprang into action.

Our stripper was just superb and even if we all knew that our husbands and partners wouldn't be over-impressed, we all had a wonderful day. It was never a sordid party and certainly not as the newspapers described it — they also said I have these parties every other weekend.

I've had to endure a lot of unpleasant comments about this occasion, but be reasonable — I am sure that in other parts of the world women have such parties and invite male strippers along. The party commenced at 2 pm and ended well after 5 pm, so there was a lot more to the afternoon than what was shown on television. We learnt about the diet product and had a guest speaker from the distribution company.

The *Sunday Telegraph* had got in on the act on the weekend before Episode Six was screened, with this silly, sensationalist article. It talked about: '. . . saucy, sexy stuff at the Donahers' ' and: 'a naughty knees-up'. They'll use anything to get people to read their paper, I suppose.

# SYLVANIA WATERS—AND THE STORY CONTINUES WITH NOELINE'S GIRLS-ONLY PARTY

This burly black stripper was a popular lad at Noeline's hens' party — but Laurie was less than impressed...

# 'Laurie, I think I'd better tell you something'

It's saucy, sexy stuff at the Donahers' this week when Noeline lays on a bit of light-hearted amusement at a girls-only bash.

Before long, the bush telegraph in Sylvania Waters does its stuff — and the bush are overly impressed. LIZ VAN DEN NIEUWENHOF reports:

## Striptease caper leaves menfolk underwhelmed

THE tongues are working overtime in Sylvania Waters after a naughty knees-up at Noeline's after Laurie's.

Problem is, Laurie is nowhere in sight when Noeline invites some of her female friends over for a festive bash. Entertainment is provided by a beefy black stripper who has the girls whooping with his saucy antics.

Noeline, never backward in coming forward, is more than happy to report on the terrace she gives it to him straight.

"Laurie, I think I'd better tell you something. While she gets Laurie to before you hear it from someone else," comes the opening gambit. Then follows an apologetic appraisal of the day's events.

It's all hilarious stuff — and we had this large negro stripper. He was beaut!" Noeline continues, between loud guffaws.

Later, after her inebriated friends have gone home, Noeline has some

knowing how else to respond, he censoriously blurts out. They smell!

"And he didn't have a hair on his body."

But there's more talk of sex when Paul and Diane launch into a discussion about how they hear of the outrageous goings-on at Macintyre Crescent and have their

Paul, of course, hears it all from girlfriend Diane, who had been invited to the girls-only romp.

He seems unsurprised by his mother's high-jinks. "She's a typical blonde," he mutters disparagingly when told of the stripper.

Although somewhat disapproving of all the goings-on, he's reluctant to make an issue of it.

has affected their bedroom exploits.

Diane coyly admits to sister Megan that they've disregarded her doctor's advice to abstain from sex for six weeks after Kane's birth.

"Paul is such an animal — he makes it hard for me," she squeaks.

Young Michael, meanwhile, is being rather subdued.

won't be deterred. "And he didn't have a hair on his body."

Laurie looks dismayed. "Wouldn't you like a white man with the same body?"

There's a slight pause and then, not able to reply, Noeline weakly parries with: "But Laurie, you can't get them like that."

Laurie, in turn, doesn't quite know what to make of this.

First comes an uncertain smile. Then, still not

Indeed, he seems content to play the piano — displaying some talent and withdraws to his room, where he desperately tries to conceal some perfumed letters he's received from a friend in England.

Then, just as you think the Donahers are about to slip into a kind of normal family mode, Noeline springs another surprise.

This one's a whopper — and we won't spoil it for you. You'll just have to wait until Tuesday.

Noeline: "he was beaut!"

Most of the men, including Paul, were not impressed although Laurie didn't seem to mind too much when I told him later and showed him the photos. Michael summed it all up in his commentary when he said: 'The females were mildly excited and the males were rather strongly jealous. Personally, I don't get off on that kind of thing'.

And they had to show Laurie commenting about black people, right in the middle of the party scenes. This happened on a completely different occasion and at a time when we thought the cameras weren't rolling. In fact, Laurie was just having a general discussion with the crew on the subject. But that's what you all got to see — something controversial. This was another blatant case of their editing. I know we knew that they would expose the entire family, but not in this selective way.

Then they showed us all out having a wonderful time on the boat — all except Paul and Dione that is. Everyone knows what time we leave on Sundays if we are boating. The rules are: everyone is welcome, be at the boat at 9.30 am, bring something for lunch and bring your drinks. Kate from the BBC informed Paul and Dione that they were the only ones not out on the boat that Sunday and then you saw their reactions. This was a classic example of the crew running from one to the other like small children: 'Dione, Noeline said this . . . how do you feel about what Noeline said?' It's like fishing, isn't it? Bait the hook, toss it into the water and see what comes out.

They also had to show us climbing into the

rubber-ducky in an intoxicated state. I suppose they didn't screen the rest of that lovely day at the club and on the water because it would have put a lot of viewers to sleep.

Then we were over at Paul and Dione's. Paul showed everyone the holes in the bedroom wall, caused by Dione pushing him during an argument. This created so much trouble for Dione — her brother was very angry with her and telephoned to say his piece. He eventually hung up on her and it left Dione in a state of shock.

It was never a joke about us having a foster child — Laurie and I looked into the situation for a very long time. We agreed to let the film crew come along to the Dr Barnardo's Home, and they gave us permission to do so. I was so upset by the visit: all those poor young souls with so much hardship in their short lives. How sad and heart-wrenching; the occasion was a real eye-opener for both of us.

The best part of Episode Six was Michael playing the piano.

\*     \*     \*

The publicity was becoming very distressing by now and when I received this tardy little letter I crept away and cried. What or who would go to the trouble of buying an envelope, paper and a stamp to send this?

*Hey Drunk*
   *They say the big black fella got right up you.*
   *Tell us what you got — a house, money, boat,*
*but no happiness, that's why you drink.*

Whoever this person is (and I have had three letters, all pretty much the same), please don't waste your money. Perhaps my advice should be to go and get a job and make something of yourself. You obviously need help and I have more to do with my time than read your filthy remarks.

# EPISODE SEVEN

## Tuesday 1 September, 1992

E PISODE Seven dealt mainly with the subject of my dear little Michael's (the big
teddy bear) sixteenth birthday.

One afternoon during the filming Laurie and I
had been having a blazing argument about work,
and it followed us home from the office. We had
no sooner arrived home than the crew just walked
in. Laurie was very annoyed by the fact that they
hadn't even knocked and screamed at them go
away. They left the house, but I know for sure
that they kept on filming from outside. We ended
up having a heated discussion about Michael's
sixteenth birthday party. Our personal commotion subsided, as it always does, and after dinner
Laurie asked the crew whether or not they had
been filming. Of course, the answer was a definite
'no'.

Brian Hill later told me he was only keeping the
crew busy when they were filming us talking
about this party — who would want to see us
organising Michael's birthday celebrations? But

the story was now about to unfold on the TV before my very eyes.

You can call me bitchy or nasty if you like, but when someone like Brian had been in my home for that length of time and had conned me so convincingly and exploited us, no wonder the public and journalists were writing and saying such things about us. Me especially.

Michael can think what he likes, but in this series he had too much to say, and as I have explained before, when my kids can't get their own way they blame poor Laurie.

Yes, deep down I did want Michael to have a very memorable sixteenth birthday party, and yes, had there been 90 young people I would have coped, and so would Laurie have coped. In my haste many weeks before, I bought four pads of invitations and gave them to Michael, so he can't take the entire blame. He must have been in heaven! 'Mum's bought all these invitations, so I'll do my best to fill every single page.'

Laurie has this way about him of getting hold of a magazine when the pressure is on and burying himself in it. But when these incidents were being filmed we thought they would never be shown. The problem is that Laurie always wears my very feminine reading glasses when he's doing this and he looks ridiculous — with them on. Don't you think someone would have advised him to take them off? Too much to ask, obviously.

There was a very big discussion regarding Michael's party, but in the end I came to the same conclusion as Laurie. We didn't want any trouble, or the gatecrashers that Michael suspected would come. For Laurie, his home is his castle and we just don't have the money to repair or replace things that are ruined or broken. On the other hand, I always try to see my kids' point of view and sometimes I do think Laurie is very severe. But no young person, be it 10, 13 or 16, has the right to be disrespectful to any parent. So, even though it is pretty important for a young man to have a sixteenth birthday party, I took Laurie's side on this event of the year. I had no alternative but to go along with the head of my family.

Laurie is the mediator; he's a good man and bears the brunt of all the things my children do. He's not their father, but when you read the papers (not that I would ever again believe anything I read) and see the documentaries about what stepfathers can do, my kids were so lucky — so very, very lucky.

In the end we had a great family night for Michael's birthday instead of the big party he'd planned. Even Paul had a good time.

Paul and Dione began to talk about their wedding plans in this episode. They started with the idea of a registry office wedding, but Dione later said she'd like to have the ceremony at our house.

My Paul, to me, is one in a million in many ways. He is a very good dad to Kane, even if he is hard on Dione most of the time: he can be very overpowering. But he is a good father and I only hope that this will continue in the future.

\*     \*     \*

Talk about the *Young and the Restless!* This *Sylvania Waters* was becoming just as bad and most of you who were viewing the show were in a quandary. I was too. I was amazed at how this series was still making prominent positions in the papers and had to ask who was paying for all of this? I sincerely hoped it was not my taxes, which are astronomical. Boy, oh boy! But don't you think that by that stage our friendly little directors were up in the clouds. You see, we were a very small price to pay, considering their names appeared at the end of each episode.

What else could there be to show you all? By now you all knew that I was lanky, brassy, bottle-blonde, crass and uneducated. What were they doing?

I guess all I am saying is that I am sorry, so very sorry. Firstly to my husband and family, and to all the people of Australia. Yes, I feel the same as you — it is an insult to call us ambassadors for Australia. In many ways it is our fault, but in more than many ways we are not responsible for this outcome.

\* \* \*

By this time we had the *Bass and Flinders*, a cruise boat, gracing our private waterways. Oh yes, dozens of people. The captain would come up the canal and point to our house. At first he got this wrong and pointed at our beloved neighbours' house, but was later corrected.

Our local paper ran an article on this under the headline: **STICKYBEAKING AT THE STARS**, and the *Sunday Telegraph* had a similar piece, entitled: **VOYEURS AHOY!** The *Sunday Telegraph* article said: '. . . Obviously the couple —

and more publicity-shy neighbours — will have to watch over their back fence, as well as the front, for any nosy intruders.' They weren't wrong!

On Saturday mornings it was like the local high street out front and the canal was busy with sightseeing boats. Imagine how you would feel?

# EPISODE EIGHT

## Tuesday 8 September, 1992

BY this episode I was absolutely fed up with the continual plot of showing Paul's abode — no money, so poor, etc — and then straight over to our home and all its splendour. Well, Laurie and I are not 27 years old and let's see what class of home Paul has when he has reached our age. It won't really worry Laurie and myself, for we will be long gone.

The whole crazy show seemed to be about proving to you all that we have money and give nothing to anyone, but this is where it was so wrong. Paul and Dione have said on several occasions, and I quote: 'Noeline is very good to us'. That must include Laurie, as he is my partner. Perhaps he doesn't know about everything I've helped Paul and Dione with, but he is aware of the majority of things.

Before Episode Eight went to air, though, Laurie had his say in the *Sunday Telegraph*. The article was headlined **SYLVANIA WATERS: THE STORY GOES ON — BUT THE 'STARS'**

**AREN'T TOO HAPPY. LAURIE CRIES FOUL OVER ABC EDITS**, and went on to explain our point about the selective editing of the series. There was also a piece on Paul and Dione — **PAUL AND DIONE ADMIT SHOW CAUSED A 'RIFT IN THE FAMILY'** -- which talked about the tensions that the show had caused. We were all under a lot of pressure.

In this episode we decided not to take a Dr Barnardo's foster child. No, I guess I will stick with my three little problems and my extended family. I think it's enough.

We also talked about our wedding overseas. This was very important to me. I am not getting any younger and I guess that being such an insecure person, it was a comfort to know that I had a permanent partner. I am very proud of Laurie and to marry him would make our years together complete. The reason we chose to marry overseas is that we only ever wanted a small wedding and it was our marriage, not one of the children's.

Many curious people have written to us about the wedding, so this is the time to tell you what happened. After the plans to marry in Monaco, and the preparation Laurie did with the consulate here in Sydney, we were informed when we got to Nice that it was not going to happen quite the way we had planned. We were most upset and I guess when the family found out that we were not able to get married there they might have thought: 'Great, now they'll marry back here in Sydney'.

We continued to enjoy our holiday and on our return we did get married: on 13 June 1992. As

# SYLVANIA WATERS: the story goes

# Laurie cries foul over ABC edits

By NIK GARIFALAKIS

L AURIE Donaher, the patriarch in the real-life drama Sylvania Waters, has slammed the ABC and the program's producers for misrepresenting his family in the series.

In an exclusive interview, Donaher also admitted he was once charged with assault after ramming a garden hose down a neighbour's throat, smashing several of the man's teeth.

Speaking from the office of his contracting business, Donaher said the 12-part drama — which has become a hit since its debut in July — was inaccurate because several family squabbles were taken out of context.

"It's been blown out of all proportion. I think it should have been called 'The Rich And The Poor', the way they have shown it."

Donaher said conversations were edited midway through and rearranged at the producers' discretion, without consulting the family.

"Certainly we said some of those things, but they were said at different times," he said.

"There was a lead-up to it or something said after it — not just the particular sentence they might have used.

"They have just tried to create something that really wasn't there. It was there, but they're making it a lot worse than it was. It was very selective editing."

Donaher admitted yesterday he had been charged with assault after a dispute with a neighbour when the family lived at Mortdale.

He said he had been threatened and, in defence, had rammed a garden hose down the neighbour's throat, smashing some of his teeth in the process.

"It was 15 years ago. It goes to show we are quite normal," he said.

Donaher was charged with assault in a Sydney court and fined.

> **6Up until then, everything had gone quite nicely. As soon as we asked them for something, they said no9**

"I'm sure anyone in my position would have done exactly the same thing," he said.

Donaher said relations between the family and the ABC had been tested since the series went to air.

His family had asked to view the entire series before it was screened, but was turned down.

Requests that the family name not be revealed were also ignored.

"We asked to see the tapes after it was finished, but they wouldn't show them to us," Donaher said.

They were never to use our name, and they did on the very first night. That's when we started to worry.

"They mentioned our business, which we didn't want them to - all those sorts of things.

"Up until then, everything had gone along quite nicely with Channel 2 - they were our friends.

"As soon as we asked them for something, they put the brakes on and said no."

Harry Bardwell, an executive producer at the ABC, said it was the network's policy that the Donahers not receive tapes before the programs went to air.

"They have seen a number of screenings, but not the whole program, and we want to control its transmission," Mr Bardwell said.

"We don't want copies going out to the press in advance."

But Mr Bardwell admitted that selective editing had helped create a more dramatic effect.

"There's no denying that what you are seeing is a concentrated version of their lives, and it has been selectively edited in order to heighten the drama of their day-to-day existence.

"It's also true that sequences are juxtaposed that did not necessarily happen directly after each other."

Mr Bardwell said an agreement between the Donahers, the ABC and the BBC was made before filming began last year.

The Donahers had the right to request that the cameras stop rolling at any time, but had no say in the editing or post-production stages.

"I don't quite understand what Laurie's complaint is, actually," Mr Bardwell said.

"There may have been something in there that Laurie said that he regrets."

Mr Bardwell said public criticism may have forced the family to cry "foul".

"Obviously, there are times when the portrayal of the family has been criticised extensively in the press," he said.

"Consequently, one deference is to say that the way it was edited is not the way that they really were."

The Donahers now want to reveal the true story of the making of Sylvania Waters - but at a price.

"We are waiting for someone to come and offer us

Laurie Donaher: says scenes were taken out of context

some money and we'll tell our story," Laurie said.

"We have had heaps of people who have wanted us to do stories. Anything we say to them they will play back to us and ask us to help them edit it.

"That is not what happened with Channel 2, unfortunately."

Interviews with Laurie, Noeline and their children are fetching between $2000 and $3000, according to their agent, Brian Walsh and Associates.

With the series to debut in England later this year, the family can expect to be paid a small fortune, which television insiders predict will finance Laurie's car-racing venture.

Mr Bardwell said British audiences were already talking about the program, which was destined to be a hit.

---

planned, we had our closest friends but no family. I became Mrs Noeline Donaher and I am very happy. This is just something that my children are going to have to adjust to. After all the years Laurie and I have been together, and all the ups and downs we've had, they will have to understand that I am very happy — most of the time. It is also very hard not to retaliate when they slam my dear husband, or blame him for every little thing. Much as I love all my clan, they have

# on — but the 'stars' aren't too happy

## Paul and Dione admit show caused a 'rift in the family'

SIX months under the television microscope has taken its toll on Sylvania Waters' battlers Paul and Dione Baker. The young couple, who even shared childbirth with an estimated 1.5 million viewers on the reality-TV documentary, have found it tough coping with their new-found fame.

By JULIE NANCE

Paul and Dione with baby Kane: 'even a simple trip to the supermarket can turn into a nightmare'

After the joint ABC-BBC production documented their lives, even a simple trip to the supermarket can turn into a nightmare as shoppers recognise the "woman who talked about sex" and "that Paul bloke".

"If I had seen, or the family had seen, all the tapes before they went to air, I'm sure there would have been a lot more fuss kicked up about showing them," Dione said on the ABC program Couchman last week.

"Honestly, it has caused a slight rift in the family. It hasn't made our lives completely sunny.

Approaching its eighth episode, Sylvania Waters has become a big talking point at dinner parties, on buses and in offices around the nation.

As the petty jealousies,

backstabbing and drinking are shared with strangers and friends, Noeline, Laurie and their extended clan attract names ranging from "cringe family" to "suburban shame".

Dione, pregnant when the show first beamed into viewers' loungerooms, now sits with baby Kane and husband Paul, a 26-year-old Telecom worker, "frightened" as each episode goes to air.

Although admitting the show is an accurate reflection of their lives, Dione says she wasn't happy about being forced to talk about sex in front of the camera.

"They made my sister come over and they

made us sit down and have a discussion about sex. I never talk about that subject with my sister," Dione said.

"The whole time I was sitting there eating, I was so nervous. I had to stop laughing because I was shoving things into my mouth.

"Most of it (the show) was real... a lot of it was out of context. Some things were said once, but shown three or four times in different episodes."

With real-life family dramas on Sylvania Waters often outstripping the scripted soapies, some viewers have been a little confused.

Paul, in particular, is often singled out as an actor.

"Our life has changed a lot, I think. At a second job that I do, cleaning, I am forever being recognised," said Paul, who recently moved out of his Mortdale home with his family.

"Dione and I went shopping once up at Hurstville and that was just incredible — we had to leave the place because so many people recognised us.

"I don't think I'd say I'd never do it again or 'I wish I never did it'. Sometimes you say 'I wish I never did it'. For all the exposure and things that have come out of it, I am glad I did it in a way.

"As I say, people backstab you and you finally get to see what they have been saying about you."

Strapped for cash and surviving day to day as

best they can, Dione and Paul's life is far different from Noeline and Laurie's who enjoy all the splendours of a million dollar, canal-front home.

Because they are seen as Mr and Mrs Average, they usually get positive feedback when stopped in the street. People say "We can really relate to you guys" or "You are so brave to have done some thing like that."

But Dione said she would hate to be in Noe-

line and Laurie's shoes, because they were copping the most flak.

She said they at least had the advantage of being able to tell the crew to leave if they were being too intrusive.

"If they were giving us the poops, we'd say 'Just go away, we don't want to see you, just leave'," she said.

Tension in the series often erupts between Paul and stepfather Laurie.

"We won't always be in harmony — some other shows may show families always in harmony," he said.

"That's not true, because you always have your fall-outs, especially with step-parents and stuff like that. You aren't always going to agree.

"I just take it with a grain of salt. If I see Mick or Laurie or my brother or my mum saying something nasty about me, it's nothing that hasn't been said before."

to realise that I love the man I am married to. So, if my family read this book, just remember — be kind and don't criticise Laurie.

There was a lot of talk about the behaviour of children in this show, most of which concerned Michael. Despite the problems that Michael and Laurie sometimes have, Michael did say that he feels, deep down, that Laurie likes all of them: Paul, Joanne and himself.

The eighth episode was cut short by about 10

minutes and you were all probably left hoping that the ABC darkroom had a fire and all of *Sylvania Waters* had been burnt, but that was not the reason at all. This is what happened.

One afternoon when filming was in progress, Michael came home from school completely out of sorts and went straight upstairs to attempt to do his homework. I went up to ask him how his day had been and he was very snappy and edgy. A while later there was a knock at the front door and I answered it to find a lady and gentleman standing there. They complained that Michael had hurt their daughter on the bus coming home from school. He had twisted her arm and they wanted to have a word with him.

Michael came downstairs and it took about one minute for him to become argumentative. His attitude was appalling — he had no respect for these concerned parents. Had I been the gentleman I would probably have landed him one around the ear, but I also knew the cameras were filming the whole thing and for me to jump up and down would have been even worse. The couple were, by this time, very irate and voices were raised. Michael was completely out of order. I went to get Laurie's assistance, but he was having none of this one. By now, the lady had noticed the cameras and questioned the producer, so the couple said what they had to say and left. I said a few more choice words to Michael and sent him packing to his room. He, of course, had his reasons, but to be so rough to a young lady was just not good enough.

The entire noisy conversation had been filmed,

but once again we were assured that this was not
the right ingredient for a documentary. We thought
'so be it'. They wouldn't tell us a lie, would they?
Oh no!

We later read in the paper under a headline
**SYLVANIA WATERS LAWYERS TV BAN** that
the parents in question had taken legal action to
prevent the ABC from screening this part, and I
wondered how they managed to get it stopped.
There were a lot of people who appeared on the
show that the ABC didn't get a signed release
from: one being my daughter, Joanne.

\*     \*     \*

I was sitting in my kitchen one day around this
time when the phone rang. For the next hour I
thought I was going to go off my head. A lady
from the *Telegraph* started to explain that she
wanted to read an article to me, written by one
of their journalists, about Laurie. It was to be
printed in that Saturday's paper. I first asked how
she got the number and was told that she obtained
it from a file in the office. This could not have
been true, as our phone number is unlisted. She
must have had some good contacts.

This sub-editor started reading and before she'd
got further than 100 words I was crying. My
world was crashing in on me. There I was, alone
and listening to this article. I was in one hell of a
state and when I protested about a couple of
things, it only made it worse. Some time before,
our red BMW had been stolen and here was this
woman telling me what they were going to print
about the incident.

I was like a small child — cringing and crying

as I listened to all this hype. When she finished I asked what this had to do with *Sylvania Waters*. Why were they so intent on destroying our entire family? Did our parents and grandchildren have to know all this? She replied that we were now public property and our lives would never be the same again.

I implored her not to do this awful thing to us and asked her to have a heart. Did she not have a family whom she loved? I was still hysterical and asked if they had so much information on Laurie, what did they have on me? She said that they had it from a very good source that I'd been a madam a few years ago. Had the conversation not been so upsetting I might have had a laugh, but what I heard was tragic. The end of this story is that she went to the editor and they eventually decided to run the article later, under the heading: **LAURIE'S COURT FIGHT OVER BMW**, and in a very toned-down form, thank goodness.

*       *       *

By the eighth show I had given up and was convinced that this would never improve. I was a shattered human being and nothing will ever erase the humiliation I felt.

> *Brian, before you went home to England, you confided in me by saying that people would not particularly like me. That was a gross understatement: detested me would be more like it, but you said that by the fifth show was over things would improve.*

At about this time I received the following letter from a Sylvania Waters family:

*I have watched a few episodes of* Sylvania Waters *and am absolutely disgusted. Firstly Noeline isn't Australian, she comes from New Zealand. She is so common, and thinks she is above the rest of us. I am ashamed to live in the same suburb that she does. You are not a typical Australian family at all. The British think that we are a pack of ockers and you have just shown them we are that and worse. My daughter spent twelve months over there trying to convince them we are not behind the times and we are a refined lot. Well after* Sylvania Waters *they will think she has been telling them a pack of lies. No one in their right mind would give a child to a drunken woman like Noeline and a slob like Laurie . . . the only decent one amongst you is Paul, Dione needs to grow up . . . Heaven help us when the series is shown in the UK, they will have a field day laughing at us. My daughter is writing to say we are not like you thank goodness.*

For the miserable $13,999 and the thought that our family could do it as a fun thing, this had, as Laurie and I often said, been blown out of all proportion.

# EPISODE NINE

## Tuesday 15 September, 1992

THIS was one of my favourite episodes, for it covered so many different aspects of the family and our day-to-day living. There was Laurie stocking the bar fridge and cleaning the boat, myself and Pat chatting in the kitchen, Mick building a garage and all of us talking about Paul and Dione's forthcoming wedding.

This was more in line with how I expected the show to turn out. It showed unhappy and happy times, with a bit of drama, and was a pleasure to watch, especially as it gave an overall coverage of the family. The music was also very light-hearted. More thought was put into the music than what the show was doing to our feelings.

Showing Mick making his very first cup of tea was great. I guess no-one could be that thick, but I can tell you that if it was not for Yvette, Mick would not survive.

On the down side, this episode was probably one of the worst for my so-called 'drinking problem'. Quite a lot of the show was devoted to

# Battling the bourbon

By LIZ VAN DEN NIEUWENHOF

WE'VE been served generous helpings of just about every problem that could possibly visit a suburban family since our first introduction to the Donahers of Sylvania Waters.

And just as we've been lulled into the belief — mistakenly I hasten to add — that there is just nothing left to keep us titillated, up pops Noeline with a zinger.

She has, we're told, a certain unhealthy affinity for bourbon and Coke — sometimes eight glasses a day. Now she doesn't think she has a drinking problem, only an unquenchable need to b͟ʳͥ⁻

Noeline in her kitchen: problems with parenting

Mick Donaher

‹ I don't think I'm a drunk but I think that at times alcohol doesn't agree with me ›

showing me with a glass in my hand (especially as halfway through we slipped back to New Year's Eve), but what the heck. In fact, at times after watching the series, I think that maybe I do have a problem.

To make things worse, the *Sunday Telegraph* had run their usual preview on the Sunday before this show, with the headline, next to a photograph of me, **BATTLING THE BOURBON**.

This ninth show demonstrated quite clearly what I have been saying all along about the editing of the series. There was more of the same: contrasting us and our lifestyle with Paul and Dione and how little money they have.

Would the public outcry have been so intense if this was the sort of material that viewers had been seeing throughout the series? No, I really don't think so.

I thought that this episode was witty, humorous and not hurtful to anyone. Why couldn't there have been more like it?

# EPISODE TEN

## Tuesday 22 September, 1992

THIS episode continued to play one lot off against the other, but this time it was Laurie against myself. What were they thinking of?

We were all keyed-up over the wedding, with everyone wanting to make the day the best we could. The teamwork from neighbours and friends was remarkable and this was all for the wedding of my son Paul to Dione, whom I care for very much. Things were tense in the house: Laurie wanted to do this, and I wanted it this way. Just the general humdrum of a garden wedding.

I'd read the Sunday papers and knew what was coming up in this programme, so I had to do my utmost to stop Laurie from watching. The newspaper previews explained that Episode Ten contained a rather private conversation between Michael and myself about Laurie, and also showed Laurie and I arguing in the kitchen. (Despite his declaration back in August to avoid the whole thing, he had been watching some of the shows.)

I engineered a little scheme. I gave Laurie a huge baked dinner that night, knowing full well that he would lay down afterwards and fall asleep, which he did just like a robot. At roughly 9 pm I stirred him and wished him a good night, and like a little lamb he toddled off to bed. I sat and watched the tenth show with Michael.

The entire segment on Laurie and I arguing about how to cut tomatoes and what we'd had for dinner was staged. How could I be so unlucky that they would screen this?

On to Dione's hens' night. This caused another little tiff with the directors. One of the guests had a little too much to drink and Joanne got really hot under the collar and asked the crew to stop filming. When Joanne attacked Brian he said he'd told us it would be warts and all, but they packed up their equipment and left. I later took Brian aside and tried to persuade him not to use any of the footage of this incident. The entire crew thought it was funny, but if it had been one of them I'm sure the idea would have lost its appeal.

But there it was for all to see — the guest who was practically asleep in the restaurant. We can thank our lucky stars that they didn't show her later in the nightclub when she was totally asleep on the table. Anyway, it was a great night and Dione will remember it for years to come.

There was more about Michael's dirty hair in this episode. Again, I couldn't work out why the viewers would be interested in this.

We also talked about Paul and Dione's wedding and what to get them for their present. Paul actually said that Laurie and myself are always there for him, even if he has said some bad things.

One of the main issues of Episode Ten centred around a very serious conversation between Michael and myself about Laurie and our arguments. Laurie was conveniently not at home that day and the conversation was instigated by the directors. Brian had called Michael downstairs and directed his line of approach, but he assured us he wasn't going to use this segment, as it was only a documentary.

It was a shock for Michael and myself to watch this. Later, Laurie could not work out how we could have been placed in this situation, knowing Brian and Kate as well as we did by then.

Brian was devious in his planning, whereas Kate was much more honest in her direction. If she wanted a little more spice she would direct the questions accordingly, but Brian — well, I never worked him out. Okay, we were now getting more and more letters of support, but I could have been left in a very sticky situation after this episode.

These are some of the lovely letters we received around this time.

From Susie of Rostrevor, SA
*Dear Laurie and Noeline*
*I am sad that media and viewer feedback has caused you and your family so much distress. You have all given us so much pleasure and entertainment over the weeks, you deserve better.*
*You exposed your lives, yourselves and your relationships with amazing courage and honesty.*

*The least we can offer in return is gratitude and a large measure of courtesy. Please be assured that the many who do not speak up regard you all with affection and pride.*

*I'm sure, although the critics are loud and vocal, they are in the minority. Also, they probably have deep-seated problems with their own integrity and self-esteem. They see your honesty, caring values and refreshing ability to enjoy life as a threat.*

*You are true Aussies — open, unfettered and guileless, and many of us out here love you for that. You reflect accurately our own joys, difficulties and efforts on behalf of our families.*

*Noeline, you are fantastic!*

From Paul of Mundaring, WA
*Dear Noelene*
*I am writing to say I have watched your TV programme each week and can only say I have enjoyed being a 'fly on the wall' in your household.*

*I think you are a great family, both unpretentious and earthy yet successful.*

*As usual the Australian public love to 'pull down' and denigrate anyone who succeeds, and in my opinion a lot of adverse comments are jealousy as you have a nice house and boat etc. What I admire most is your ability to tell your family you love them. If only half the people watching could express their feelings as you do, then we would live in a much better world.*

*Keep on just as you are, and ignore the 'stuck up' pretentious critics who probably have all manner of skeletons in their own wardrobes, if the truth was known. Thanks for the programme.*

From Susan of Newtown, NSW
*Dear Noeline*
*After all the bad press you've received, I wanted to write to tell you that you have a fan in me.*

*We are very different in many ways, but I can appreciate your good points.*

*You're a kind person who gives the impression that you'd do anything for anyone. You're generous and honest.*

*I like the way you seek to have meaningful relationships with people by asking them what they think about lots of things. For example Pat about your drinking, and Michael about you and Laurie. You're brave, because you still ask questions even when you may not want to know the answers.*

*You can see the funny side of things and enjoy having fun.*

*I do hope that life will settle down for you all. Thank you for sharing your lives with us. I loved watching* Sylvania Waters *and will miss you all.*

*God bless you Noeline.*

\*     \*     \*

I can see now, after careful consideration, just how the directors got us into situations and caused us to say things on the spur of the moment that we later regretted even if they were true. The directors obviously weren't happy just with the trouble they had already caused between Paul and Laurie. I wonder how they can sleep at night, considering how low they have stooped to create a show like this.

After watching this episode you could clearly see how these people create their so-called hits. It is obviously at the expense of the people being filmed and without any regard for what damage they do, even though it might be the truth.

I believe that the bond between Laurie and myself is strong enough to withstand this sort of sneaky, underhanded skullduggery. I think the two English directors will be quite amazed to know that our family has somehow survived all of this. I am sure that when the filming was finished, and they were on the plane back to Britain, they were taking bets as to how long we would stick together. Well, I have news for them. We will still be together long after their marriages and families are on the rocks. Maybe they might like to come back again some day . . .

*       *       *

I made a note in my diary that Michael said, in no uncertain terms: "Mum, that was a very dangerous assignment". But, being completely at the mercy of the directors, our trust was to be betrayed once again.

# EPISODE ELEVEN

## Tuesday 29 September, 1992

THIS episode focused on Paul and Dione's wedding — a day to remember for us all. When my family pitch in and help, they do just that — they are the most loyal and loving clan, including my sister, Annette, and our very good neighbours, Allan and Pat.

We all know there is a lot of preparation for such things, even if it is only a garden wedding. Annette and Yvette were at the house bright and early, flowers were being pinched from next door and the entire lot of us, except Michael, were trying to make this day perfect for Paul and Dione.

My darling Laurie, even though he did object to this and that, was out cleaning the windows and putting satin ribbons on the boat, which was the wedding vehicle. He had been up very early cleaning down the pebble-crete and making sure the pressure was not too much for me. By the way, Mick even put the tablecloths on the food tables — another little job he'd never had to do before (what would he do without Yvette?), but he did it perfectly.

Dione's mother arrived to do the normal thing and see to her daughter. At this stage I don't think she knew that Dione was going to wear a long gown and when I went upstairs and heard hot words between them I came back down so fast. Being old-fashioned, I feel that you can only be a bride — a traditional bride — before you have a child. But this is 1992 and life has changed for everyone. (Let me tell you that my life has changed for ever.)

Dione looked like a doll all dressed up: so lovely. She looked just so beautiful, and I am very proud of this young lady who has come into our lives and produced my magnificent first grandson.

Let me make something very clear. The wedding was to have commenced at 1 pm but, with all the confusion caused by my fine-feathered friends, the directors, the celebrant thought it was 3 pm. *They* caused the confusion, not the celebrant. Mr Hamilton was just so marvellous, and on the day of Paul and Dione's wedding we asked him to perform our wedding celebrations when we returned to Sydney, even though we thought we were getting married in Monaco. This poor celebrant had a lot of explaining to do to his superiors as a result of the confusion.

Paul and Dione's wedding was perfect in my mind. Everyone enjoyed themselves and may I say that Paul looked super in his tux. I could not have been happier.

By the way, despite the agreement that Joanne was never to appear in the programme they did film her at the wedding. Even though she complained to the ABC afterwards, this episode showed brief shots of her. I also have a photo of the wedding day from *TV Week* with Joanne being captioned as Dione's mother!

*       *       *

On the same day as Episode Eleven went to air, an almighty fuss broke out over the comments of Mr Brian Howe, the Deputy Prime Minister and Federal Minister for Health, at a health conference in Canberra. The papers reported him as saying that my drinking, smoking, betting and eating habits were a result of my social class, and that '. . . people from disadvantaged backgrounds were generally worse off health-wise.' He was also quoted as saying: 'Noeline admits she has a drinking problem, wants to give up smoking, has a close relationship with the TAB, and is constantly vacillating between Gloria Marshall and creamcakes.'

Mr Howe did later fax a 'standard' letter of apology, but I still feel that he should have apologised to me personally.

Although I never actually wrote to Mr Howe, these were my thoughts at the time.

*To Mr Brian Howe*
   *It is only because I was brought up to show respect to my elders that I say 'Mr'.*
   *Well, Mr Howe, weren't you a brave man. You picked your speech, which no doubt you didn't even write, and you too got on the bandwagon. I could see it pleased you immensely when, after*

**DEPUTY PRIME MINISTER AND**
**MINISTER FOR HEALTH, HOUSING AND COMMUNITY SERVICES**

Parliament House
CANBERRA ACT 2600

Telephone: (06) 277 7680
Facsimile: (06) 273 4126

Noeline Donaher
c/- Mr B Walsh
Level 26                                                3 0 SEP 1992
500 Oxford St
BONDI JUNCTION   NSW   2022


Dear Noeline


I am sorry that you were offended by my remarks about
you at the Public Health Association of Australia
Conference on Monday.

My intention was to use the program in which you
featured as a means of making a general point about the
relationship between social background and the health of
groups of people in Australia.

I deeply regret any offence to you and apologise
unreservedly.


Yours sincerely

BRIAN HOWE

*giving me a serve, the participants at this confer-*
*ence laughed at your remarks. Out of the comments*
*you made, the only one you got right was about*
*the cream cakes.*

*If it had been at all possible I would have*
*slapped a summons on you, but I guess the best*
*way to help this deplorable feeling I have is never*
*to vote for Labor again. I have been a Labor*
*supporter all my life, but three votes that you will*
*be losing are mine, my father's and Laurie's*
*father's.*

*Mr Howe, don't think I will forget you and the*
*embarrassment you have caused me. I cannot*
*believe a Member of Parliament could come to*
*such a low point. I feel you are the rudest man in*
*Australia, without an ounce of respect for me.*

*I have consulted the best solicitors on this matter*
*and it seems that, being a politician, you are*
*protected to a high degree. But, to me, you are a*
*relentless and very rude man. I question your*
*apology also, considering you were in Sydney and*
*the fax came from your Canberra ofice. You have*
*staff, like mine in my little hard-working business,*
*that have the sanction to sign your name.*

*PS: I am still waiting for your personal apology.*

There were dozens of articles, letters and comments (and some amusing cartoons) in the newspapers after Mr Howe had made his 'apology'.
The radio stations were full of it too, with most
people coming out in our favour, for once.

Looking back, I think that the whole Brian
Howe affair was the turning point in the Australian public's thoughts and attitudes towards

us. With the help of Jana Wendt and Channel 9's *A Current Affair*, I feel that this incident did more harm to Mr Howe's career than anyone could imagine, yet it brought us thousands of supporters. So, to Mr Howe, I say thankyou very much.

\*      \*      \*

I received scores of letters of support after this incident, from people of all ages and from all over Australia.

Here are two of them.

From Sheila of Moonee Ponds, Victoria
*Dear Noeline*
*I have been watching* Sylvania Waters *from the start and have become increasing appalled at the hostility generated at you in particular.*

*I've been prompted to write because of the unbelievable speech by Brian Howe. The Labor Party is supposed to represent the working class, not treat them as a lower species. If Brian Howe wants to talk about drinkers and gamblers let him refer to the high flyers of commerce, who play the stock market and live their alcoholic lives (and adulterous ones).*

*I believe you are a very typical Australian family who work hard and earn your enjoyment. Of course you haven't got a drinking problem — if you have, then most of the country has.*

*I think you have had a raw deal from the Australian public and the media. You've had a tough life and you've made good. Just remember that. One day it will be behind you.*

# SORRY! IT'S NOT ENOUGH

Noeline and Laurie Donaher with Mr Howe's faxed letter yesterday . . . 'it looks like a standard apology'

## Noeline rejects apology

By JASON OFFORD and JUSTIN COOMBER

NOELINE Donaher, the star of Sylvania Waters, last night rejected a faxed apology from humbled Deputy Prime Minister Brian Howe.

A fuming Noeline said she was offended by the letter, signed by Mr Howe, who had blamed her drinking on her working-class origins.

She did not believe Mr Howe had written the letter and felt insulted.

"It's not like he's retracting anything at all," said Noeline.

"It looks like a standard apology letter. It's got the date stamped on it and they just shot my name up there at the top."

The Sylvania Waters housewife, who has brought the country's second most senior politician virtually to his knees, said she will only accept Mr Howe's apology if "he says it to my face".

"He said it in public and he should now take it back and he should apologise in public to me," she said.

"Why did he pick the Sylvania Waters show and our family as his topic?

"I'm not a drunk. He was saying I'm a second-class yobbo and a second-class citizen."

Continued Page 4
Editorial — Page 10

From Margaret of Darling Point, NSW

*Dear Noeline*

*I and several friends aged 35-65 watch Sylvania Waters and we all think you are great. We enjoy it but know what happens when they film interviews, long or short, and edit out the bits they don't want. The ABC filmed the police at Redfern for a long period, but when the film was screened they showed none of the good things done by the police.*

*Your family all come across well and are certainly interesting and attractive.*

*That terrible Mr Howe does nothing for the country — he only takes taxpayers' money. He caused the doctors to strike and, as one radio man said, the doctors do more for the country in a day than Howe does in a year.*

*You are a very attractive, intelligent woman and should have your own TV show. My friends and I like you all, especially your younger son.*

*Best wishes for your future health, happiness and success.*

# EPISODE TWELVE

## Tuesday 6 October, 1992

A T last, the night of the final episode. It seemed like a lifetime since the first show. Who would ever have believed all this carry-on about a Channel 2 documentary?

By now, though — and partly thanks to Brian Howe — a lot more people were in our favour. Even some of the TV critics were writing good things. The *Sydney Morning Herald* TV guide had been particularly flattering, saying, among other things, that: 'In 11 weeks, Noeline and Laurie have become the most famous pairing in Australia. We are fascinated by them . . .'

Even Dame Edna seemed to like us! The *Daily Telegraph-Mirror* ran an article on the day the last show was screened, under the heading: **DAME EDNA LOVES NOELINE**.

This last episode was no different from the first — still in the same vein of the rich and the poor, and they showed Laurie and I arguing again.

Even when Laurie and I were about to leave the country to get married and have a well-earned

Barry Humphries yesterday . . . 'The Labor Party has always been snobs' Picture: BOB BARKER

# Dame Edna loves Noeline

**EMBATTLED** Noeline Donaher of the real-life TV soap Sylvania Waters has found a new champion — the world's best-known housewife, Dame Edna Everage.

"She might even become a character in Sylvania Waters who visits and gives glamour tips to Noeline," said

By SUE WILLIAMS

Barry Humphries, creator of the jet-setting Moonee Ponds megastar.

" 'Noeline', she'll say, 'my son Kenny will design a few frocks for you'."

Humphries, in Australia to promote his autobiography, sat up all night watching tapes of the show.

And now he's entered the spat with the country's deputy Prime Minister Brian Howe on Noeline's behalf.

"I think Howe's mistake, poor man, is that he didn't know whether he was talking about a real person or Mrs Mangel," said Humphries.

"The borderline between fiction and fact is becoming very blurred, particularly in Australia, with the dreamtime in which we all live.

"It is a strange turn of events where a Labor politician is making disparaging remarks about the working class. No Liberal politicians ways been snobs."

Humphries called for Noeline to be included in the honours list.

"Move over Dame Edna! Here comes Dame Noeline! Edna must look to her laurels with a new housewife megastar in the pipeline, ready to step into her slingbacks."

holiday, Paul arrived with Dione in tears. The next thing was that everyone was uptight and agitated and I was in tears. I would have thought that Paul could have stayed away and let us depart happily, but no, once again there was drama over nothing. (Probably, though, he should have been coming overseas with us.) Anyway, we all tried to forget the misery and have a bit of fun and a few drinks with some friends and the family at the airport.

*     *     *

For the evening of the last episode we planned a barbecue with a few close friends and the neighbours. We had also agreed to have Channel 10 present to film the reaction from us after this final show. I think we were all a little sad that night because it had been a big step for us, and Laurie and I had grown quite fond of watching our children on a Tuesday night at 9.30 pm.

I was visibly very upset after the show. I had obviously bottled up a lot of my feelings and emotions for the last 12 weeks. After being asked a number of questions I broke down and cried. There were probably some tears of joy as well because, deep down, I was very proud of my family. My decision almost 12 months previously to submit us all to this documentary was, despite what some people might think, a huge personal success for me.

All that remained for us now was to live in hope that Channel 10 would televise, through their show *Hard Copy*, that final night with all its happiness and sorrow as it actually happened.

# GUIDE PREVIEW

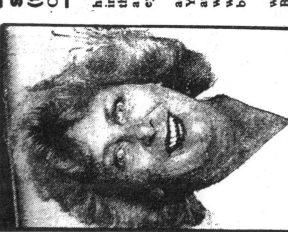

Noeline ... the blue eyes of a Sylvania Waters darling.

## SYLVANIA WATERS
### (final episode)
On ABC-TV at 9.30 pm

IN 11 weeks, Noeline and Laurie have become the most famous pairing in Australia. We are fascinated by them. To be honest, Noeline is a bit of a darling. Those are fabulous blue eyes. That is a great TV face.

You may have missed the original advertisement. "Any Dramas In Your House?" it politely urged. "We are looking for ... a lively family with something to say, who are willing to let us into their lives ... better than a soapie, this is real life."

The ABC was touting for the BBC, which had done something similar in Britain. There were 100 replies. It took less than an hour to whittle them down to five. The Donaher-Bakers were always odds-on.

Tonight is the last we shall spend at Sylvania Waters. Noeline goes to the races and jumps to her feet to shout home a winner.

A woman tells her it is not done to stand up in the members' enclosure. Thankfully, Noeline knows the correct form. "I told her to get stuffed," she says.

Finally, it is Mother's Day and Noeline and Laurie prepare to fly away to Monaco, where they plan to get married after 13 years.

They are arguing about in-laws. Dione and Paul are having a tiff. Mike has problems with the car. Michael has agreed not to stray as far as Kangaroo Point.

Suddenly they're gone. The jumbo, caught from a great angle, climbs into the afternoon sun. It's a bit of wrench.

Brian Howe must have been off his rocker.

**Robin Oliver**

We prayed that they would not edit to create sensationalism as the ABC and BBC had done throughout the series. Channel 10 promised they would show it as it was and, to their credit, they did.

The interviewers and crew from Channel 10 were very thoughtful. They could see that I was upset and did not push too far with the interview. They left us in peace, and for that I do thank them.

We had a great barbecue on that final Tuesday with our friends, the Channel 10 crew, people from the *Daily Telegraph-Mirror*, our Manager, Brian Walsh, and his assistant, Chriselle Rodgers. Everyone was happy.

\*　　\*　　\*

I received these letters after the screening of *Hard Copy*.

> From Frances of Rooty Hill, NSW
> *Dear Noeline*
> *I have watched every episode of* Sylvania Waters *and last night's screening of* Hard Copy *which has prompted me to write a short note to you and your family.*
> *I really enjoyed every episode of* Sylvania Waters *and you should not be ashamed of your publicity. You did a marvellous job and should be very proud of what you have achieved.*
> *You must remember that obviously the BBC were looking for a special family that had a lot of drama and special events arising in the near future to prey upon. (Could you imagine how boring some people's lives are and how they would have been televised?)*

*DRY YOUR EYES, STOP FEELING GUILTY AS YOU ARE A LOVELY WOMAN, HAVE A WONDERFUL FAMILY AND YOU HAVE MANY, MANY YEARS AHEAD WITH THEM TO ENJOY. YOU DID AN EXCELLENT JOB AND I THINK YOU HAVE MORE ADMIRERS OUT THERE THAN YOU THINK AND THOSE WHO AREN'T ARE JEALOUS.*

From Jo of Northcote, Victoria

*Dear Noeline Donaher*

*I watched your life unfold on the TV with great amusement and laughed with you, but I wasn't laughing tonight when I saw your tears on the Hard Copy show. You had the guts to apologise to your family for hurting them and for that I **really** admire you.*

*Every day in every household across Australia and the UK scenes go on just like the ones in your home filmed by the TV cameras. By allowing the cameras into your home you have certainly **not** ruined your life but have opened up the possibility of limitless enrichment. Your family relationships have come under the microscope and all the areas that together you can work on now are apparent to you. You are one of the most fortunate families I know of because now you can work together to communicate your love for one another really effectively.*

*Allow this whole experience to be a turning point in your lives for a very positive future with no need for regret.*

*With very best wishes to you and your family.*

From Peter of Chelsea, Victoria
*Laurie and Noeline*
*As an average Aussie, as you are, I must say
I loved your show but I can see it has had a
terrible effect on you all.*

*I am watching* Hard Copy *at present and I
feel terrible to see Noeline so devastated by it all.*

*I'm 41 years old and would like to think I
represent another average Aussie by saying I could
read between the lines. I looked forward to seeing
you all weekly and I will sincerely miss you all
now it's over.*

*You are all average lovable Aussies and I respect
you all. I hope you go on to make millions from
appearances and I certainly would welcome you
to my home anytime.*

*I loved Paul and Dione, Michael and Mick,
his wife, your neighbours etc and the show. All I
can say is not all Aussies are so shallow as to
condemn you. I respect you all.*

*Please have a great life.*

\*　　\*　　\*

And this is the final word on the series — from
my diary, and dated 6 October 1992.

*You must appreciate the feeling I have tonight. It
is finally coming to an end, or is it? Does this
long, dreadful nightmare end tonight? I have been
told by Page Lovelace from ABC Publicity that it
may rear its ugly head again when the series is
shown in Britain, but all I know is that for now
tonight is the end.*

*It has been like riding a roller-coaster — since
it started there has been no getting off. The*

Noeline and Laurie Donaher watch the last episode of the ABC's Sylvania Waters at home last night. Picture: MARK WILLIAMS

# Noeline weeps as series ends

### By PHIL McLEAN

AS Noeline Donaher watched the last episode of Sylvania Waters last night she cried "years of relief", grateful that the warts-and-all documentary series had ended.

Surrounded by family and close friends, Noeline became emotional as she watched the credits roll for the last of the 12 weekly ABC TV programs.

Noeline and husband Laurie threw a barbecue to celebrate the last episode with 30 family and friends.

Noeline laughed and cried throughout the show.

When it was over she said, "I was crying tears of relief.

She vowed never to do a program in the same way again.

"I wouldn't do anything like that again unless I had full editing control of what was finally shown on TV", Noeline said.

The Donahers filmed a Lotto commercial yesterday.

The television advertisement, which has Noeline and Laurie squabbling over whether it was "number 30 or 31" which came from the Lotto wheel during a draw, is expected to be shown from October 16.

Last night the British creator of Sylvania Waters defended his view of the Donaher's lives.

Principal executive producer Paul Watson, from London's BBC, said he and his team had made it clear to the Donahers before filming began that camera crews would be present in the household regularly.

Proudly displayed on the pool table of the Donaher's home are more than 30 letters of support Noeline has received following an exclusive interview in the Daily Telegraph Mirror.

Ironically, tonight's gathering was filmed.

Channel 10's Hard Copy will feature the barbecue.

*amusement it has given all of you; the tremendous agony it has given me; and the hurt that has been caused — all because of this stupid woman who made the most costly phone call of her life. It has been like a volcano exploding: insulting the people who have viewed it and embarrassing, to the greatest degree, me and my family. Tonight it will all go away.*

*My tears are not those of a person who accepted a contract and didn't like what she saw. It is the deceit and the destruction and heartbreak is has left us with. It is the cost of the loss of my only daughter, Joanne; the humiliation to my family in New Zealand and to everyone who knows me through our business or personal life.*

*I am not proud of what I have done. I am not a hero for what I have done, but in this life you either sink or swim and if any critic, or anyone who knows better than I, wants to crucify my remarks, so be it. But before you pull this tale of my life to pieces, please respect my views. I am a wife, mother, stepmother and grandmother and a very hard striver. I care for the world we live in and I strive to make life easier for everyone. I don't want praise, but hell, I don't want any more criticism.*

*If I have offended you with my displays of racism and crudeness, let this be the final curtain. Perhaps you can all leave us alone, unless you have something pleasant to say.*

*Looking back on Sylvania Waters, all I can say is that if I was asked to do it again, I can* assure you the answer would be NO!!

# In Hindsight

*Now that it is all over, here is the last word — from Yvette, Dione, Laurie and myself.*

# YVETTE

## November, 1992

THE phone rang one morning and it was Noeline. 'Guess what I've just done,' she said. I said: 'What?' She proceeded to tell me that she had been listening to the radio and had heard that they were looking for an interesting family, so she had rung and they were coming on the following Tuesday, to check us out I suppose.

The lady that came was Chris Pip, a researcher for the ABC. Chris proceeded to tell us what they were looking for in their interesting family. She took photos and told us what would be expected of us during the six months of filming. When Chris left, Noeline knew deep down it would be our family that they would choose.

A few weeks later we got the news that it *was* us. It was quite a shock, especially for me as I am very camera-shy. I thought: 'Oh, no! What am I going to do now?' But that was that, and we were the ones to be filmed.

Later in the week we went for dinner at Brighton to meet everyone — the producers, directors and the film crew. As the night went on and more was discussed about the expectations of us, and the money we would be receiving, a few of the family members were not impressed at all. In actual fact it was very close to being called off, but after talking and discussing between ourselves we all agreed, bar one family member, that we would do it. It's not every day you get chosen to do something like this.

Later the next day, the producer and crew came to our work to see what was in front of them and then they decided to come to our house. I nearly died, because I knew that the kids' beds weren't made and the place was a bit of a mess. I jumped in the car and took off — flew all the way! I made the beds, cleaned up and prepared myself to show them around.

They arrived, I showed them the house and they asked me about my family and background. I told them that my dad is Russian and my mother Dutch; that I have two sisters and a brother; and that Mick's mother lives with his brother. They thought it was good that I had a different cultural background and said they would probably film at places like my grandmother's at Easter, because it is celebrated differently from the normal Australian way. My father was preparing for bypass surgery and they said they would probably like to follow me to visit him. None of this was ever filmed.

Well, the filming started — rotating from house to house, but they visited us less than the others. I suppose they knew from the start what they really wanted and I guess we were just not as controversial as the others. We didn't talk or argue about other members of the family. I think we just didn't open up quite as much as the others, who trusted the crew as friends and didn't think that what was being said or done would be included — at least not for 12 whole episodes.

The crew would ring and ask what we were up to that day. If they thought they might get something, they would come. They wanted to know if we had to go to the hairdresser's or out shopping. At first I didn't tell them because I was too embarrassed to go out with them following me. Mick was quite different. He didn't mind at all and Kristy and Lisa became quite close to them.

They would arrive, have a coffee and biscuit, discuss things and then film. Not much would be done at our house, so they'd pack up and leave. When they asked about family members and I answered (it obviously wasn't what they wanted), they'd try to put words in my mouth, but I wasn't going to fall for that.

I was not going to discuss family problems with millions of viewers, but, as we have seen, others did. We now know that Mick and myself were filmed only because we were part of the family. They were more interested in Laurie and Noeline's lives; Paul and Dione's problems, such as lack of money; Paul's attitude towards Laurie; and Paul and Dione being new parents.

So time went on, and when the filming was finished we were all invited to the ABC for drinks and the viewing of a 20-minute promotional tape. What a shock! We were all pretty stunned by what we saw — arguing, drinking, the bitching and so on. I could not believe that out of six months of filming this was what they had put together. They could have shown more of the many nice times, such as Lisa's third birthday party, which was at her pre-school with all her family and little friends. But no, they put in 20 seconds worth. What about all the days on the boat, the dinner parties, the children playing or being bathed? Our pride-and-joy car was stolen and they came and filmed us virtually in shock. As I said before, they came for 'warts and all', but they showed all the warts and left out the good times that every family has.

We all left the viewing a bit frazzled, but thought the rest must get better. The big day came — the first episode. Boy, was I nervous. Mick went to see his dad in the afternoon and the street was crammed with reporters and photographers. It was very uncomfortable for Laurie and Noeline, so they decided we would all go out for a quick bite to eat, then come back to our place for the show.

It started, and didn't we all get the shock of our lives! We all sat in disbelief. That night I went to bed and cried my heart out. I couldn't believe it. Mick said it would get better, but it didn't.

Every Tuesday the nerves would set in for what we were going to be faced with that evening. We usually watched the show with Laurie and Noeline, or with our friends Greg, Debbie, Lyn and Dean.

It got worse and worse every week. Noeline was a wreck: she couldn't believe what was happening. The press had a field day with it and also with

Laurie and Noeline's lives. It was absolutely unbelievable. What we thought was such an innocent thing turned into a nightmare for them.

When it was all over the bagging didn't stop. People's lives were still being torn apart, and all because of selective editing. As time goes on, life is going back to normal — because things can now be said between us the way we want them, and not given to the editor to play havoc with.

Laurie and Noeline have appeared on several TV shows, which gives them the opportunity to counteract all the bad publicity they have received. Paul and Dione love the attention they get, because they were made out to be the poor forgotten children of the wealthy family by the water.

Mick and myself just sit back and watch as the others lap up the limelight. We are returning to living normally and going to work to keep what we have worked bloody hard for during the 11 years we have been together.

# DIONE

## November, 1992

I guess Paul and I were pretty excited when Noeline first spoke to us about our chance to be on television (which, by the way, is all I felt it was going to be). We had no idea of what was to come in the next six months, or what havoc it would cause to our usual 'easy come, easy go' attitudes and lifestyle.

It all started for us in November 1991 — a month that I would dearly like to erase from my memory forever. We both thought it would be a blast and maybe even profitable, but little did we know we were to be exploited beyond our wildest dreams. My mum had warned me from the start, saying it would be an invasion of our private lives and that I, not so much Paul, would deeply regret it when it was all finished. Things just moved too fast for me to take heed of her advice. Now I guess the saying 'Mother knows best' truly is a fact.

Joanne, Paul's sister, said it would be a great

chance to get some money to buy a house, and considering that I was seven months pregnant the idea sounded fantastic. Paul and I agreed to meet, along with the rest of the family, all of the ABC/ BBC people who were to be involved with our lives for the next five months.

We met at a restaurant in Brighton and talked for a couple of hours about this 'documentary'. We felt it would be a great experience for us all, and also that the programme would enable us to look back on six months of our lives.

Towards the end of the night Joanne had a disagreement of some sort with Noeline: I think it was over the amount (which was $13,999) we were to be paid, or something to do with Laurie. I'm still not sure, as we were all pretty tipsy that night. Anyway, Joanne got up and left the restaurant *very* upset. Paul rang her when we got home and it was then that she advised us she thought it would be best if she just stayed out of the whole thing. She said that the easiest way for her to do that would be to move out of her mother's house. Paul protested and begged her to reconsider, or to stay with us for a while, but she had already made up her mind and found somewhere to go. Somewhere that she could be out of the camera's prying eye.

It hurt Noeline a lot (Joanne is her only daughter) to come home that night and find a note saying that Joanne had moved out and wouldn't be coming back. I felt horrible and I think it affected all of us. On the first day the crew went to film at Noeline's house there was a huge fight between Paul and Laurie. Paul was defending Joanne's wish not to be involved in the programme. Unfortunately, this was to be the first of many disagreements between the two of them. The crew thought this would be a great opportunity to start filming. Another argument broke out, but it was decided to let this one go as it was personal. This was only the first of many such days, but one that caused a lot of damage to the relationship between Paul and Laurie.

Being Paul's wife, I have to admit, is a hard job. He has a short temper and can fly off the handle at the click of the fingers. I guess, from what I've heard, that he and Laurie are pretty similar in many ways that neither of them realise. Paul has, I think, rejected Laurie since the first day he stepped into Noeline's life.

I know that the directors and producers were aware of this animosity, so they played on it. Whenever Paul had the shits and one of the two directors was present, they would ask Paul to talk about Laurie. It used to shit me no end watching Paul open up to these strangers. I would confront Paul after these 'bitch sessions' and say that he was starting a rift in his family, and that he should think before he speaks next time. I don't think he ever listened to me, or sat down and really thought about any damage that he could have been doing. We both did and said things so innocently and unknowingly.

It used to make me angry, knowing that these people just didn't give a shit sometimes. It was easy for them — they could all go home and live their normal lives, while we would be left with the aftermath, trying to live our lives 'normally'.

But then I guess we were all pretty gullible and said things we didn't mean; things that, once this was over, we would all regret. We had no idea what the end result was going to be, or that the family would never be the same.

Then there was the birth of my beautiful son to endure. The crew wanted to be with me, watching every contraction, every tear, every breath. In the beginning I was all for it, but when the big day finally arrived just the thought of them waiting at the end of the corridor in the labour ward gave me the shits. Fair enough — when it came down to it I had the final say, but the female director would not let up. In the end I had to get Paul to tell her to get out and stay out until my baby was born. Any woman who has been through childbirth would agree that the last thing you want while you're having a contraction, or trying to push, are sound and camera guys listening and watching.

It wasn't until after my son was born that I discovered they had been filming and recording the sound outside my door for three minutes prior to the birth. At first I was severely pissed off. I thought 'How dare they?', and 'How embarrassing'. After I'd seen Episode Four (the programme in which Kane was born), however, I realised how wonderful it had turned out. I will cherish that episode forever.

When I came home from hospital after the birth the crew were all over us like flies, although I can understand this. They wanted to know what it was like to be new parents, how it had changed our lives, and, more so, had it affected our outlook on life? It was good, because even though at times we couldn't bear the fact that they were coming over, it did give us the chance to get things off our chests.

Four of the crew had children and it gave Paul and I the opportunity to talk about our experiences, and even pick up helpful hints. The assistant producer, whom Paul and I got on very well with, even gave us some great clothes that his little boy had grown out of. So, please believe me that we did have some really good times during the filming. We seemed to get on really well with the crew — one day they brought food and drinks over and we had a big barbecue. They even cleaned up after themselves. Yeah, they were great in a way.

It wasn't their fault that the show ended up the way it did, or how it portrayed the family. Basically (besides all the fighting) that's how we all really are. It did cause, however, a lot of tension between my mother, my brother and myself. They were totally against it from the start, but it was not until after the showing of Episode Six (where I talked about sex after childbirth with my sister) that I was to receive their full fury. My brother rang me from Perth to say how disgusted and embarrassed he was with me. I didn't get a chance to defend myself. Then, when I saw Mum at work the argument got so heated that I eventually told her where to go. I had never spoken to my mother like that in my whole life, and couldn't speak to her for weeks afterwards.

I truly believed I had disgraced my family and I ended up hating the show for doing this to me, to my family and my marriage. Yes, after only five months of marriage, Paul and I had become near enemies. We were at a point where I just wanted to leave. I blamed the ABC and the BBC, but I also blamed Noeline for involving us all. I should have just blamed myself, but in the state I was in all I wanted to do was to take Kane and hide.

I couldn't understand how Paul had loved the whole thing, or that he wanted to do it all over again. This got up my nose and it took a very long deep and meaningful conversation with Paul to get my head straight about what was happening to us all and, even more, about what was to come! It's hard for me to do 'celebrity' things now, whereas Paul loves all the attention. It still doesn't make sense.

There were times during that summer of filming when our house was hotter than an oven. On one particular weekend the crew came over while we were sweating heavily and told us that Noeline, Laurie, Mick, Yvette, Michael and their friends had gone out on the boat. This really gave me the shits. Here are Paul and Dione sitting extremely hot and bothered on their lounge, so stupid me decides it's about time I said something, so I did. The crew must have thought all their dreams had come true. I sat there and blabbed for an hour. I usually tried to stay out of these bitch sessions, but I guess they got me while my guard was down.

When Paul and I eventually watched that episode I cringed at what I had said. I felt as if I wouldn't be able to face Laurie and Noeline again. The funny thing is that it wasn't until I had a conversation with Yvette that I learned that she and Mick are hardly ever asked out on the boat. They just turn up on the day. That made me feel about ten times worse. Noeline did, in the end, make our lives a lot more comfortable by giving us some money for a second-hand air cooler for that hellhole we used to live in.

Paul and I had been discussing marriage while I was pregnant, and even more so now that Kane Alexander Baker had arrived in our lives. We want the best for our son, and seeing that Paul and I love each other very much we decided yes, we would get married. Now all it came down to was where and when? It was hard making these decisions as I practically had to work around my mother. I'm not saying that she's difficult, it's just that she wanted no part of this documentary from day one.

This reminds me of when I was in hospital during the birth. As soon as Noeline or the cameras appeared, Mum would disappear. She blamed Noeline for the whole thing, seeing that she had volunteered our family. Not only did I have this on my mind while in labour; I was also desperately trying to hide my tattoo, which Mum eventually did see. Actually, she coped better with my tattoo than having all the cameras around! When Paul or I tried to explain anything to Mum about the series she would protest and all but block her ears.

Back to the wedding. Leading up to the big day, Paul and I had the crew with us all the time. They even filmed us on our bucks' and hens' nights. Let me tell you, it was hard trying to explain to my friends that a camera crew would be with us most of the night. Passersby and onlookers must have thought we were movie stars or something! I didn't seem to notice them much that night as I was pretty tipsy and having a great time. The crew even bought me a present for my so-called 'kitchen tea,' and I'm pretty sure they had as good a night as all of us girls did! Paul's night was a lot more low-key than mine, but I'm certain the liquor trade did good business that evening.

So you see, life with the ABC and BBC was not all that bad. As Noeline said in one episode, we had our ups and we definitely had our share of downs. It's just coping with the aftermath that seems to be difficult. Oh, and the wedding — as you would have seen, it was very stressful, but it did turn out to be the best day of my life, and Paul's. That, besides the episode in which Kane was born, is our favourite.

# LAURIE

## December, 1992

F OR me, the story really starts on the Tuesday
evening that we all went to a restaurant at
Brighton with the crew. Here, we were to
be informed of how much money we would be
paid, we would receive our contracts to sign and
meet the crew that would be assigned to the
making of the documentary.

In the lead-up to this night I had been told by
Noeline that she'd heard we could expect to be
paid in the vicinity of $250,000, and every member
of the family was aware of this too. I'd thought
of the consequences of doing a show like this (or
at least I *thought* I had) long before signing up, so
I was prepared to accept the worst. That was, of
course, until I was informed by Paul Watson that
we would be paid $500 a week. 'What?,' I said,
'You must be joking!' I told him that as far as I
was concerned he should forget the whole deal.
He seemed quite amazed and shocked and then
asked Pam Williams, one of the ABC producers, if

we had been informed of the amount of money. She said no.

I stormed back to the table where everyone was laughing and joking and told them all what had happened — well, that threw a spanner in the works. I was howled down. It certainly quietened things down for five minutes and there were about three groups of people from the ABC/BBC all huddled up, deep in conference.

Looking back, I suppose my attitude was one of want, but then again, if you are going to air your soul on television I think you should be well compensated. Certainly a lot more than $500 per week, and that was to be divided between seven people. Anyway, I was overruled that night and the decision was made to go ahead with the show.

I feel sure that if the rest of the family were approached again tomorrow, to do another show under the same conditions, the answer would be a firm *NO*.

From that first night in the restaurant I felt that the directors and crew probably took an instant dislike to me. I'm sure they also realised that they wouldn't get much mileage out of me, and to a certain extent they were right. I made up my mind that I would not change my way of life in any way, even in front of the cameras, and I am sure that if you have seen any of the episodes you will understand what I mean. Not at any time did I get dressed up or act for the camera and I detested wearing a microphone, which they tried to make me wear all the time. At this point I must say that I did see a hell of a change in the personalities of some family members when they were performing for the cameras!

During the filming of *Sylvania Waters* the ABC and BBC crew were very good in the way in which they did their work. You would often be unaware that they were in the same room when filming us, and this is probably one of the main reasons why the show was such a success. We became very blasé about their presence.

The five months of filming certainly went very quickly, but towards the end I could see that some of the family had had enough and were starting to treat the crew as I had from that first night. The novelty had worn off and they weren't getting enough money for the inconvenience involved.

What about the show — well, what can I say? Good, bad, embarrassing, degrading, sneaky. I think it's enough to say that the ABC and BBC achieved everything they set out to do.

It certainly was not what the Donahers and Bakers expected and, incidentally, we have never seen or heard from the two directors, Brian and Kate, since the time the show went to air. We thought they were our friends and I'd expected, when the show became such a great hit, that they would at least have written to congratulate us and themselves. I am sure that their absence on the night of the first episode was for a good reason. We also asked, on numerous occasions before the series went to air, if we could view some of the shows and were told, in no uncertain terms, *no!*

All I can say now is that they — the BBC and ABC — chose the right family for their series.

# NOELINE

## December, 1992

HERE we are just a few days before Christmas 1992. At about this time last year *Sylvania Waters* was being filmed and all that you have read is now past tense. I guess that one year down the track many of you are wondering what has happened to my clan and where they all are.

For the past month or so Paul and Dione have been having no end of trouble. Yes, the tension from the series has been taking its toll and the pressures that have mounted in their lives were almost enough to see their wedding vows reversed. Thanks to our heavenly father, their marriage has been saved and our dearest little Kane Alexander still has his family intact.

Kane, by the way, is now 11 months old and is walking, or perhaps toddling is a better word. He is just the dearest little boy. I don't see him as much as I would like, but Paul and Dione are fabulous parents.

The rift between Paul and Laurie is undergoing

163

major repair and I am so happy to say that they are now talking to one another. I guess this is mostly for my benefit, as I really stress out when there is discontent between my loved ones. I am sure we all realise now that our beloved friends from the UK set the trap, and having been given enough rope to hang ourselves, we did just that. As I have already stated, I will be damned if I will let the BBC destroy our family and this time next year all the bad memories should be gone.

I wasn't so lucky with Joanne. Although her little note said she would come home after the filming, that was not to be. Her father has moved from Sydney and Joanne is now in her own unit and perfectly happy. This is enough for me — her happiness and safety will have to do and at least we are talking on a healthy basis now. Paul has also been re-introduced to his grandmother, so all in all things are balancing themselves out.

Joanne, as I have mentioned before, has a very strong will: obstinate is how I would describe her. But I love my little girl with all my heart and I know she knows this by now. I also believe that our children are only loaned to us and go on to become our dearest friends as we grow older.

Michael. Well, his report for the end of this year is not much better than last year's. Unfortunately, due to the scarcity of money, Laurie, Michael and I have agreed that Newington College has to come to an end and Michael will continue his schooling locally. I am sure that my dearest younger son will thrive, though — at heart I know that Michael will succeed in any venture he puts his mind to.

What about Mick and Yvette? They have stayed pretty much the same, although Yvette experienced enormous strain while the show was on. That beautiful, striking smile has returned and life at their home is back to normal. They've had problems with a neighbour and their pool filter, but the latter is now fixed so their Christmas should be a happy one. Kristy and Lisa are still the same beautiful little girls and I love them.

Over the past few months Laurie and I have appeared on a few television shows and done some interesting things, but I suppose the knockers will say that my last words on the *Hard Copy* show were that I did not want any more publicity or notoriety. Well, I endured all the bad publicity and by going on television we have shown you all that we are totally normal people — not actors reading a script, but normal, everyday people who created the monster with their own hands.

Many kind people have asked how our business is going. Well, we are still there and still plodding along. Although the series was the reason behind the decrease in our business, perhaps our clients saw through the editing too and felt for us. I think that many people have realised that we were foolish to do something so stupid, but have allowed us another chance. Yes, we (and especially me) *were* foolish, but our honesty in business is unquestionable and we have total loyalty to our clients. To all of our clients, a sincere thankyou for this second chance.

We have received a great deal of publicity and mail, both good and bad, since the series ended.

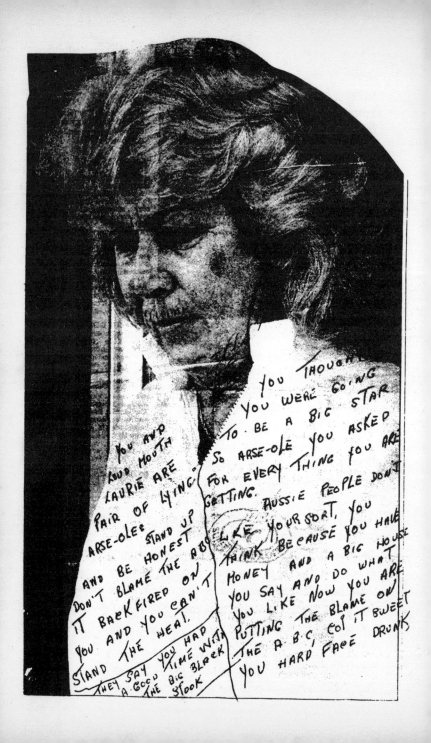

Most of the letters have been in our favour, but we have had to put up with some terrible things from some very sick people.

*       *       *

There is one more point on which I would like to set the record straight. This is regarding the article about Laurie's ex-wife, Judy, which appeared in the 5 December 1992 womens' magazine, *New Idea*. There was a photo of Laurie and I on the front cover (**SYLVANIA WATERS SAGA CONTINUED . . . THE *FIRST* MRS DONAHER TELLS: 'NOELINE STOLE MY HUSBAND! I SHOULD HAVE PUNCHED HER EYES OUT!'**), and a two-page article inside the magazine.

We went out with our friends on the boat one Sunday and had a lovely day. When we came back home for a cup of coffee, Laurie turned on the television to see an advertisement for that week's *New Idea*. There were our faces being flashed across the screen and panic went through my body. The voice was saying: '. . . Noeline stole my husband . . .' and I felt the same panic as on the night of the first *Sylvania Waters* screening.

What was this, so many weeks after the show had finished? Tears filled my eyes and the old saying that Laurie's mother told me came to mind — 'Hell hath no fury like a woman scorned'. I want to get this story straight.

Many years ago, before I met Laurie, I used to go out with my girl friends on Friday nights to the Kareela Golf Club, and it was through this club that I eventually met a blonde lady called Judy. She always appeared very stable and happy and although we did not become friends, we spoke on a friendly basis. My conclusion was that she was in the same boat as myself — separated with kids and trying to make it alone in the big world. I had no idea at that stage that she and Laurie were connected.

Then some months down the track I met Laurie, who (the little devil) was adamant that he was divorced: his story about his 'ex-wife' was very convincing. He never denied that he had two wonderful sons, though. After all of this, I concluded that his marriage was over well before I came on the scene and, as I have already mentioned, we decided to live together.

Now, it was stated in the *New Idea* article that I called Judy to ask her to have Laurie's clothes ready so that I could come and pick them up. This was not me. Laurie had always been 'good with the women', and this must have been one of his previous encounters.

Of course we hurt a lot of people when we moved in together, but no-one has had the decency to tell my side of the story. Laurie and I hadn't been together long when he decided he was missing his boys so much (and Judy too at that stage) that he felt he had to go back to them. I remember being in shock but went to the kitchen and called Judy to explain the situation. Laurie left me that day, a Friday, and I was pretty sure I had lost him. I was heartbroken, but if this was his decision I had to go along with it — I could not have lived with myself if I thought I was keeping him away from his boys.

I didn't know what to do — we had rented a

house and started our contract labour business together, and Laurie had gone. That weekend Laurie arrived with a magnificent bunch of flowers and seemed happy with his decision to leave me, although he did hold me in his arms and say how much he missed me. He left, and I cried all that day and night. On the Sunday, Laurie rang and asked me to come and have a meal with him and Judy, for he wanted us all to be friends. This was too much for me to bear, so I turned the invitation down and went out with a girl friend to cry on her shoulder instead.

By the Monday morning I had decided that we would have to move, as I couldn't afford the house on my wage alone, but Laurie arrived and said he had made a dreadful mistake. He said something like: 'I want to be here with you and I love you with all my heart.' I did what any normal woman in love would do, and that was to take him back, despite the fact we knew we were hurting his wife, his family and his parents too.

I extended my friendship to both of Laurie's boys, who were very badly hurt over all this. I have managed to maintain a healthy friendship with Mick, but have had to resign myself to the way that Stephen feels and I respect him for it. Over the years, though, I have often argued with Laurie if Stephen has needed anything, such as a loan — Laurie has been the one to say no, but I have said yes.

Stephen has always been polite and will come to the house if I invite him for a meal or whatever. I am sure I am not his favourite person, but he tolerates me — the article said that Stephen has never liked me, which I think is a little unfair. It's also hogwash to say that I don't like Laurie to call round to Judy's home to see Stephen. I would never try to stop Laurie from seeing either of his sons: I'd get nowhere with him if I behaved like that.

Please bear in mind that Laurie and I have been married for only six months. For 13 years before that we survived on our love and trust for each other. I am sure that there were countless times when he thought of leaving me, especially because of the pressures my three lovely children put on him, but we had the best ingredient for a good relationship — love.

I'm not being picky here, but the article mentioned how often Laurie and Judy talk on the phone. As Laurie says, he could count these occasions on one hand and I know he is telling the truth. This is the second important ingredient of our relationship — trust.

The article hurt me very deeply, for there have been numerous occasions over the years, such as birthday parties for Kristy and Lisa, when we have all put aside our differences for the sake of others. This brings to mind the time when Stephen was savagely beaten up, some 18 months ago. As soon as Mick rang with the news, we were on our way to the hospital and I am sure I cared as much as any family member. His injuries were horrific! One evening after visiting Stephen, Laurie and I were driving to a restaurant to have a meal with Mick and Yvette and I thought of Judy being on her own. I didn't hesitate to ring her, using the car phone, and we all enjoyed our meal despite our differences. Or what about the soup I made and sieved for Stephen because his mouth was wired up? Hell, this story in *New Idea* rocked me, I can tell you.

The article said: 'Judy shows every sign of overtaking Laurie in the business success stakes'. Who really cares which one of them is the best business success? I have all the wealth I could ever want with a kind and loving husband. Leave me out if being rich means just having the money.

Once again, my point is that if someone is telling a story they should get it right and not set out to hurt people. I am not a monster — I am a mere woman and I can tell you all that if I had known Laurie was married, I would have sent him packing in the first couple of weeks.

There is much more that I could say, but I don't want to affect my relationship with Mick, Laurie's son, so I will allow my respect for both of them to get the better of me.

Perhaps now is the time to let sleeping dogs lie.

\* \* \*

*To the people of Australia, I want it known that I did not undertake to do* Sylvania Waters *for notoriety or for gain. It was innocently done and I say sorry to those I have offended. I am thankful for the support I have received and will go back to being Noeline Vera Donaher — 5 feet 10 inches tall with big feet, Laurie's wife and very proud and happy to be her.*

*To my own children, whom I love, I say one final time that I am sorry for any heartbreak I have caused you. To my stepchildren also, I am sorry.*